# INNOVATING LIKE A STARTUP, EXECUTING LIKE A CORPORATION

*Solving the problems that matter most
in a data and AI-powered world*

Jean-Claude Junqua

Innovating Like a Startup, Executing Like a Corporation
Published 2020 by Your Book Angel
Copyright © Jean-Claude Junqua

Printed in the United States
Edited by Keidi Keating
Layout by Rochelle Mensidor

ISBN: 978-1-7341814-3-2

# Contents

# Acknowledgments

Writing a book requires significant effort, many hours away from the family, and much support from your friends and colleagues. It is the result of all these contributions, and though many people helped me, I will most likely forget some of them in this section. If I did, I am sure you know who you are, and I am grateful for your support, partnership, and encouragements.

I am fortunate to have a fabulous family who helped me learn and grow continuously. My wife, Yuriko, is the rock of the family and an inspiration for me to be myself. She continually provided the love and support I needed to write this book. My eldest son, Jonathan, showed me that hard work could bring you where you want to be. I remembered this when I needed the motivation to continue writing. My middle son, Samuel, taught me that following your dreams is not something that you say but something that you do. I will always be grateful for this. My youngest son, Fabien, made me understand the true meaning of empathy, kindness, and caring. It was an invaluable gift that I am trying to cultivate and improve every day.

I would not have been able to pursue my goals without the unconditional support of my family back in France. Their love and support showed me that geographical distance is not a barrier to love.

I am indebted to Bob Dobbins, a former colleague of mine at Panasonic, who provided many helpful comments and shared his knowledge and wisdom to improve this book. Ben Reaves, another Panasonic colleague who welcomed me when I first arrived in the United States, contributed to the editing process and shared many thoughtful comments. Jay Sehmbey, who took time to read the manuscript while starting an internship in Canada, gave me very constructive comments. Despite all of their help and feedback, there are undoubtedly still many mistakes remaining. However, this book improved significantly due to the contributions of these people.

I also would like to acknowledge a friend of mine and former colleague, Ricardo Teixeira, for being with me during most of the On4Today journey at Panasonic. I learned a lot from him, professionally and personally. I am very grateful that Ricardo and his fantastic family could share with me a part of my innovation journey.

Throughout my career, I worked with many organizations and teams. All my current and previous colleagues contributed in some ways to this book because I learned from them, and they influenced my journey. I also want to acknowledge Panasonic, where I spent more than 25 years and met exceptional people—including my wife—for giving me opportunities to learn and develop. The On4Today team will always take a special place in my journey. Creating this new business within Panasonic was a dream come true, and I could not have had better teammates. It did not end up as planned, but the experience gained from this project was invaluable.

Finally, I would like to thank my fellow innovators. I am learning something new every day. It is exciting to get up in the morning with purpose and passion for changing the world, step by step, for the better. Throughout this journey, I am meeting fabulous people, and I will forever be grateful.

# Preface

We are living in a unique period of history. Digital transformation and digital innovation are changing our lives. Technology is accelerating the pace at which new products and services are coming to market. Large corporations are struggling to innovate, and the rate of disruption is escalating across every industry. It is possible to start a company and bring an opportunity to market within a few months instead of years. Where do we go from here, and what does the future hold?

Having spent all my career in the innovation space, I felt the need to share the insights that I acquired through the many years working in leading-edge technology fields. I also wanted to capture personal experiences that may be useful to other fellow entrepreneurs. I love to solve problems and to learn, and this book was a way for me to pause, collect my thoughts and those of other people in the field, and point toward future directions. Startups are bold, want to disrupt the world, but are often struggling to execute. In contrast, large corporations excel at execution, but they need to reinvent themselves continually to stay relevant. However, past successes can limit them. This book addresses these challenges and how startups and large corporations can cooperate by leveraging their strengths and overcoming their weaknesses.

From my work in three countries which are very different in terms of culture, business practices, and approaches, I learned new ways to look at problems and opportunities. I also understood the importance of diversity, collaboration, and relationships. Through the experience acquired in a large corporation like Panasonic and working with many startups, I could understand the strengths and weaknesses of these two worlds, and also the gaps that currently exist with both types of organization to innovate and create new business. It became clear to me that the front-end and the back-end of innovation were often disconnected or had severe weaknesses that would prevent startups and corporations from effectively searching for new business and, when deciding to go forward with an opportunity, to execute it successfully. This realization prompted me to write this book and share my understanding, experience, and knowledge with the innovation and business community at large.

I could not have written this book without the insights and help from many people whom I connected with and learned from over the years. I wrote this book by trying to understand their wisdom and building on the top of it. As is often the case in the design thinking world, I learned how to apply the following principle: *"Reuse people's ideas and build new knowledge on the top of their ideas."* This book draws on the work of many innovators who shared their ideas through blogs, books, or conferences. I tried to acknowledge as many as possible in the bibliography, but most likely, many other contributors would also have deserved to be recognized.

As my career evolved, I moved from a pure technologist with an engineering background to a problem-solver fascinated by customer needs and how technology could help develop solutions for improving people's lives. Throughout this journey, I have been drawn to methodologies such as design thinking and lean startup, which fundamentally concern learning about the end user and using this knowledge to develop and validate customer-centric solutions quickly. I also learned how to appreciate the power of new business models and how needs and business value can drive the creation of new business opportunities.

In the last three decades, with the ever-increasing pace of change, the way to innovate has evolved significantly. From technology breakthroughs of the 1990s—which required a long time to produce results—to a focus on short-term wins and open innovation, corporations (in this book, for simplicity, I often used the term "corporation" to refer to a large corporation) have been struggling to adopt the innovation speed needed to stay relevant. Many industries have been disrupted by startups that were quicker to choose a new approach or business model. With digital transformation, software came to the forefront of innovation and many traditional corporations, often hardware-oriented, could not embrace software fast enough. Building a startup and going to market can now be done in a matter of months instead of years by leveraging technology that already exists and creating some meaningful differentiation on the top of it. Disruption can happen much quicker than before, and execution speed is critical. The power balance between corporations and startups has changed as startups can adapt faster and better to changes driven by software, speed, and iterations. However, corporations still have tremendous potential to execute and leverage their processes, customers, channels, and brand to create new business. Naturally, corporations and startups found that one of the best modern ways to create new opportunities is to leverage their respective strengths. It has led to more innovation happening via corporation-startup collaborations facilitated by ecosystems such as accelerators. Collaboration skills are becoming a must. Recognizing opportunities is becoming as important as coming up with a new idea. This book takes a look at how the innovation landscape has been evolving and provides some hints toward how it may continue to develop in the future via collaborative innovation.

Together with innovation speed, another fundamental change is in the making. Data, Artificial Intelligence (AI), and machine learning are radically changing the way people do things, redefining what is possible. Many of today's tasks can be automated, changing drastically the meaning of work and how jobs will evolve in the future. It is something that we cannot ignore as AI will transform society. This change, together with the fact that I spent more than two decades innovating with machine learning, prompted me to include a chapter about AI and how it is transforming many industries.

Though this book is primarily about innovation frameworks, I learned that people, collaboration, trust, and respect are the main ingredients of success. People are at the center of all we do and who we are. I am convinced that mission, purpose, motivation, social good, and a collaborative customer-oriented culture are critical factors for sustainable success. I tried to reflect these values in this book. Throughout my career, my interests evolved from a deep passion for technology to a strong drive for solving problems that matter and creating a better world. I also learned how to appreciate better the people behind the success, failures, and learnings that come my way. I will always be grateful for what I learned from them and for them showing me the way toward being a better person and directing my effort and skills toward creating a better world for all of us.

# CHAPTER 1

## Building a Startup: It is not complicated, it is hard, and it takes a special kind of person

### 1.1. ENTREPRENEURSHIP IS AN ART NOT A JOB

As Steve Blank, the father of the lean startup movement would say, "Entrepreneurship is an art and not a job" (Blank, 2011). Just like artists who use their inspiration to communicate ideas, thoughts, or feelings, the entrepreneurs convert their vision and dreams into a reality. As an artist, an entrepreneur is proactive, takes charge of his future and moves things along based on strong beliefs, personality, and imagination, driven by creativity and the vision of a different world.

Quoting Steve Blank again: "This concept of creating something that few others see—and the reality distortion field necessary to recruit the team to build it—is at the heart of what startup founders do. It is a very different skill than science, engineering, or management. Founders fit the definition of an artist: they see—and create—something that no one else does" (Blank, 2011). These types of people are rare, unique, and "crazy." Not everyone is an artist. Entrepreneurship is indeed art as the entrepreneurs come up with new ideas that often appear to be worthless to others. Many entrepreneurs usually take decisions that are considered crazy by the rest of the world (Steve Jobs and Elon Musk are great examples). However, those decisions often change the world.

Entrepreneurs like to take risks, and they operate in a completely chaotic system with many uncertainties and surprises. Such people are quite rare, incredibly unique, novel, and crazy. They are artists, and their entrepreneurial vision is an art. Tools, money, and excellent education are useful for founders, but until we understand how to teach creativity, the number of founders will still be limited. The human element of building a business is hard to see and to measure as it includes characteristics such as vision, culture, and values. Additionally, to start and grow a business, founders need 1) drive and passion, and 2) the skills and knowledge necessary to create a company. However, they often emphasize the latter.

## 1.2. IMPORTANT QUESTIONS A FOUNDER SHOULD ASK BEFORE BUILDING A STARTUP

As Paul Graham, programmer, writer, and investor mentioned: "Running a startup is an intense activity that never stops" (Graham, 2009). It is so foreign to most people's experience that they don't get it till it happens. The startup life is fast, which makes it seem like time slows down. The emotional ups and downs are sometimes hard to take, drawing a comparison with an emotional roller-coaster. There is no guarantee of success. It is, unfortunately, the bitterest truth about entrepreneurship. In most other jobs, success is usually directly proportional to the amount of hard work you put in, but that's not the case with entrepreneurship. Given the above insights, it is essential for the founder to be careful before spending his life savings (and that of others) and embarking on a startup adventure. It is what separates a nice idea from a great startup that has some chances to succeed. To perform this internal due diligence, the startup founder has to do some reality checks and ask the following questions:

- Are you passionate about your idea and the problem you want to solve? Do you personally need a solution for this problem? Is it a real problem?
  - For the founder to be convinced and passionate by the challenge and to want to solve a problem is a necessary condition. However, conviction and passion are not enough, and it is essential to have some evidence (personally or via other means) that it is a real pain, for which some customers would love your solution and are willing to pay for it.

- Are you ready for the startup lifestyle?
  - Being an employee from a large company versus a startup founder is entirely different. Building a startup requires a lot of determination, learnings, and hard work. There is no short-cut, and you have to be ready to invest a significant portion of your life with success often realized in the long term. Are you prepared for this?

- Do you have the needed stamina and skills?
  - Being successful in building a startup is usually due to resilience and not giving up. Do you have what it takes? Do you have enough drive and conviction to overcome rejection? Do you or your team understand the problem and the solution well enough to keep going in the face of adversity?

- Do you have a good enough understanding of the market?
  - Before spending much time building a product, you want to make sure that you have enough knowledge about your target market and the associated challenges.

- Is the market opportunity large and growing?
  - It is a necessary pre-condition. The founder needs to gather data and evidence that there is a market, and it is growing. It will also be required to raise money from investors when this time comes.

- Is this a crowded space already?
  - The more competitors there are, the more it is likely that they previously thought about your idea, that you may be already late to market or that the size of the pie that you are looking at is smaller than what you thought. Looking at the competition early on is a good indicator if you should go forward in building your startup or not.

- Who is your target customer, and do you understand how to perform customer acquisition?
  - Too many times founders focus on the solution without understanding whom they are designing for very well, what it takes to acquire customers, or what the right channels to market are. Putting some thoughts early on into the targeted customers and the pathways to market while refining the initial hypotheses as the startup progresses allows the founder to avoid early mistakes.

- Can you build a motivated and qualified team? What are your strengths and weaknesses? Can you find a co-founder with complementary skills?
  - The ability to assemble a team and to supplement the founder's strengths and weaknesses is crucial. Different skills are needed as the startup progresses. Besides nurturing relationships with potential co-founders, it is essential to be surrounded by the right people who can rise above the challenge when times are tough. It allows the founder to survive difficult nights and get through when the sea is rough. To do this, creating a culture

is very important as culture is a big part of what draws people to join startups and what keeps them going.

The above (summarized in *Figure 1.1* below) is not an exhaustive list by any means, and we could add many other relevant questions. However, in my experience, these questions constitute some of the most critical items that a founder should reflect on before going forward and embarking on the startup journey. The founder should also keep things simple, maintain focus, refrain from boiling the ocean (it is always tempting) and start with something minimal (Minimum Viable Product or MVP). One of the first tasks a founder will need to concentrate on is the identification and validation of the MVP, which is a product with just enough features to satisfy early customers.

| Questions |
| --- |
| Are you passionate about your idea and the problem you want to solve? |
| Are you ready for the startup lifestyle? |
| Do you have the needed stamina and skills? |
| Do you have a good enough understanding of the market? |
| Is the market opportunity large and growing? |
| Is this a crowded space already? |
| Who is your target customer and do you understand how to perform customer acquisition? |
| Can you build a motivated and qualified team? What are your strengths and weaknesses? |

*Figure 1.1: Important questions a startup founder should ask.*

## 1.3. COMMON CHARACTERISTICS OF A FOUNDER

Ultimately entrepreneurship is a leap of faith. Startups are hard even if you have a good team, an excellent idea, and you are ultimately successful. The most important characteristics of a founder are passion and conviction, in other words, his/her mind. If it is not strong enough, the path forward will be fuzzy, any challenge will seem overwhelming, and your startup will struggle. Your experience is useful. However, your original plan and vision are likely to change along the way in a direction you possibly never expected. Some essential characteristics of a founder are to be open to change, listening to users, and incorporating feedback. Focusing on what you can do, need to do, and what is under your control are paramount. You also have to be ready to pivot if necessary.

A founder accepts uncertainty as part of life. Will that customer sign the deal? Will this candidate come on board? Will we be able to raise the next round of funding? You are uncertain about almost everything. A founder usually creates a startup out of nothing. Whether a startup with a similar idea already exists, or it is a new idea, a startup is an organization that aims at converting this idea into a reality.

Many people will provide opinions and information. However, too much information can also be detrimental. It can create confusion, bring doubt, and create a problematic path toward decision-making. Quoting Abdo Riani, founder of Startup Circle: "Instead, startup founders should rely on several trustworthy sources (books, blogs, lectures), get equipped with enough information to take the initial steps, and acquire relevant knowledge as startup progress is underway" (Riani, 2017). Strong beliefs, coupled with the ability to receive advice and listen to others, will enable the startup to discover its way. A founder needs to be able to strike the right balance between boundless optimism and critical objectivity, which allows the founder to pay attention to the roadblocks getting in the way of the successful execution of the startup vision.

Steve Blank provided the hypothesis that founders often come from dysfunctional families (Blank, 2009), were often emotionally damaged during their upbringing, which made them resilient and capable of functioning in a permanent state of chaos. It is a reasonable hypothesis which fits quite well with the fact that to succeed, founders have to be resilient, tenacious and should have a relentless drive to succeed.

Another suitable characteristic of founders is to be driven, honest, transparent, and open. Founders will most likely change direction. Their original idea, vision, mission, plan, and strategy are likely to change in a direction they possibly never thought to follow initially. So, they need to be open to change and curious, as curiosity is an essential trait that all high performing entrepreneurs have in common. *Figure 1.2* below summarizes these characteristics.

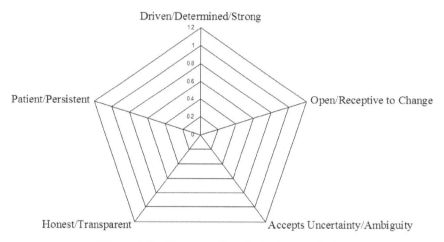

*Figure 1.2: Common founder's characteristics.*

In the end, the only way that a founder succeeds is by caring more about his/her startup than about anything or anyone else. Globally, successful entrepreneurs are exciting and courageous role models demonstrating many of the qualities required for effective 21st-century leadership. They are engaging in the art of applying entrepreneurship and intrapreneurship by:

- Developing creative ideas and innovative solutions to some of the world's significant challenges.
- Demonstrating deep values-driven conviction, creative energy, fearless and passionate purpose.
- Practicing empathy through people and customer centricity via design thinking and lean startup-like approaches.
- Constantly disrupting and challenging the status quo.

- Tirelessly coaching others to create, invent, and lead.
- Listening carefully to advisors while trusting their instincts to make decisions and following their vision.

## 1.4. A TYPICAL DAY FOR A STARTUP FOUNDER

The role of a startup founder is unique. When you are leading a young company, you must juggle diverse priorities. The strategy balances with operations and leadership balances with a willingness to listen. Though every founder has his/her way to do things, the following tasks make a typical day (see *Figure 1.3* for a summary):

- Planning to avoid spending time on random tasks which always pop up.
- Communicating with the team to align expectations, make sure everybody is on track, and discuss timely issues.
- Interacting with the startup stakeholders to talk about the big picture, strategy, and possibly investors to keep them updated.
- Focusing on the product/service by getting feedback from customers, devising with the team how to improve the startup offering and making tough decisions in terms of prioritization.
- Leading and driving growth via partnership discussions, strategic deals, and doing demonstrations and presentations to share the startup vision.
- Reflecting (often late at night) to understand what the startup could do better, faster and more efficiently and what could be potential next moves.

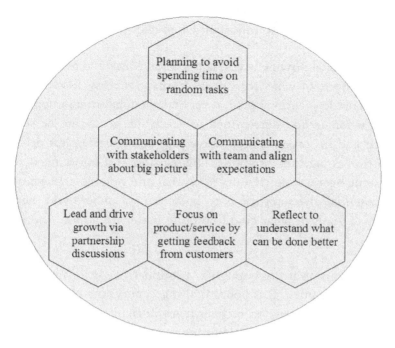

*Figure 1.3: Competing priorities from a day in the life of a founder.*

Running a startup is not a nine to five job and while not all the days look like the above, establishing a routine and carving out time to focus on and prioritize the essential items is one of the crucial tasks of the founder. It leads to efficiency and creates an impression of security inside the company.

## 1.5 THE IMPORTANCE OF GRIT AND RESILIENCE

Angela Duckworth's excellent book called *Grit: The Power of Passion and Perseverance* (Duckworth, 2016), described very well that the founder's raw talent is useful to build great achievements and develop new skills, but it requires the *deliberate* practice of these skills and additional effort. Many founders agree that this is what is needed to succeed. If you are persistent, even the most challenging problems seem to weaken as time goes on. Some also mention how much more critical persistence is than raw intelligence. It is why many people say that character was most important when choosing co-founders.

Two very well-known entrepreneurs, Elon Musk and Steve Jobs, are good examples of what grit can do to shape success. Elon Musk, an admired modern entrepreneur, is very talented, but more importantly, he is passionate and determined to reach the goals that he sets for himself and his organization. Steve Jobs and his relentless drive for perfection is another example. This passion and effort need to be consistent over a long time to reach real and notable achievements. One essential characteristic is to be systematic where you measure results, to analyze what could be done better, to adjust, and to try again.

However, passion is not enough as a founder needs to find a way to make things happen. Resilience is also accepting the challenge to be tested and the capacity to recover from difficulties. While sacrifice and struggle are parts of the journey to success, it is also imperative to learn how to bounce back. It is about rebounding and facing a challenge with a plan and conviction. Resilient people understand how to deal with uncertainty and doubt to achieve success. These are the traits of successful founders. A determined mind is a critical characteristic of a founder, and in many ways, the determination is more important than being smart.

## 1.6.  LIFE IN THE FAST LANE

For many people, the relative stability of the corporate world is attractive. For others, the opportunity to join a startup is the most exciting way to earn a living. It's hard to compare the two, as it depends on what one is looking for and the place he/she is in life and his/her career.

Working for a startup isn't for everyone. People confident in their abilities and willing to take risks tend to like startup life and its potential rewards. For many, freedom can be satisfying, but it can also be challenging. Startups give you the chance to make your work your own; however, this is often at the expense of directions. The important thing is to take ownership of what you do and to seek guidance when needed. Unlike seasoned companies, which have well-defined processes and procedures, startups are able and need to make changes quickly. To succeed in a startup, you need to embrace chaos.

At a startup, you have to be a team player, roll up your sleeves, and get your hands dirty. Your everyday activities will vary according to the situation, and some days, you may have to do almost everything. While your role will have a job description attached to it, it is common to help with whatever the startup needs. The significant advantage is that you will learn a lot and fast. At a startup, your growth will be exponential, but you are responsible for facilitating it. You are continually required to prioritize, and you are forced to rely on your strengths and improve your weaknesses so that they do not become blind spots. There is much room for change and creativity while in a large company, because of the experience and success accumulated, there is much more structure, workflows, and processes already in place, and the organization is much less open to change and new ideas.

In a large corporation, people may tell you how to do your job just because they have a high-level degree such as an MBA or a Ph.D. They may also be inaccessible because, after many years of service for the company, they have responsibilities which make them spend their days barricaded in their office. In a startup, these experts are your potential mentors and are generally accessible. For you, it is a unique opportunity to learn and grow. In a startup, you are working side by side with founders, CEOs, and the other C-level executives in the company. In a large company, generally, you have many layers of management before reaching the senior leadership team.

It will often be your responsibility to assess the risk. You will have to learn as much as you can about your company's performance and trajectory to be able, as the startup progresses, to continually assess if things are going well or not.

You will enjoy the flexibility and the ability to work from virtually anywhere, though today it is also becoming more common in large companies. You will be putting in long days (and late nights), and your responsibilities will be fluid. If you accept the job for what it is, working for a startup can be a great way to kick-start your career. At a startup, you are never stagnant, and it is up to you to get your feet wet in different tasks so that you can determine your path. Change happens fast, and, if you excel, you will quickly gain more and more responsibilities, unlike at a large corporation where career progression is often happening with time or is the result of other factors which are not under your control.

## 1.7. COMMON MISTAKES AND USEFUL TIPS

Starting a business is not easy. Every day there are many decisions to make under pressure without having the time to consider the impact of every decision. However, poor decisions can hurt the startup's potential for success. At the macro level, two main important root causes are leading to a startup failure: a lack of product-market fit and poor execution. There are also some common mistakes that startups make which impact their business negatively, or at worst lead them to failures. The paragraphs below summarize the most common ones (not in a particular order), mixed with useful tips that can help startups not fall into these traps.

- Believing that you can do it alone: Even if you are the smartest guy in the world, it will take time for you to learn it all. Looking for expertise to bring into your startup as consultants, advisors, or employees allows you to focus on the important part of the business while delegating other aspects. It is also why it is a good idea to have a co-founder to start a new business. Delegating effectively, while sometimes difficult for a founder who is used to doing everything, is key for being positioned for future success. A diverse team, including different skill sets, is critical to be able to adapt to various circumstances and ultimately to succeed.

- Doing too much and lacking focus: This is a very typical mistake. The focus is paramount for success as resources and time are limited. A startup has a limited runway and needs to execute within these constraints. While the vision can be big, one of the first challenges is to identify a niche market (often called the *beachhead* market) and to resist the temptation to go too big, too early. There may be a laundry list of features that you may want to add, but keeping the experience simple and uncluttered allows you to focus on what your users want. It is also important to build a clear strategy along with a technology and business roadmap, which identifies the focus of the company at different points in time.

- User unfriendly product: Bad things happen when you ignore what a user wants and needs, whether consciously or accidentally. It is imperative to create an optimal out-of-the-box user experience and to make it easy and convenient for users. The first impression of a product is difficult to change, and attention to details is vital.

- Pricing/Cost issues: Pricing is a dark art when it comes to startup success, and startup post-mortems highlight the difficulty in pricing a product high enough to eventually cover costs but low enough to bring in customers. For some companies, it is becoming a discipline often driven by tools and experimentation.

- Not knowing who your customer is: One vital part of startup success is understanding the problem that you are solving and who the customer is who has this problem and is willing to pay for a solution to it. It is one of the first things that a startup needs to do. This step should not be a guess/hypothesis but should be backed up by evidence and data which will comfort the startup that the direction is right. It will also allow the startup to establish the product-market fit, which is a necessary step to get the needed market testing and traction.

- Overspending: Starting a business, especially in software or Web-based services, does not require a large investment. However, some founders are sometimes too optimistic toward their cash flow, neglecting the fact that they need to adapt their directions all the time, and things do not always turn out as planned. Curbing overspending early on, even if it looks like the startup can afford it, is generally a good idea to plan for unforeseen expenses. Too much money without having a strategy and specific goals to spend can sometimes be detrimental to startup success. Money does not solve everything.

- Underspending: In contrast with the previous paragraph, underspending can prevent the company from growing fast enough. It can severely limit the potential for success as other companies can catch up quickly or even outgrow the company. In the early stage, it is generally not a good idea for a young company to be profitable too fast as it often means that the company is not taking enough risks to capture a large size of the market and outpace its competitors.

- Confusing a product with a business: What matters is having customers that are adopting your solution because you are solving a problem they have and they are willing to pay for the solution you provide to them. Even with enough customers, a product that does not generate significant traction is not a business. It is important for founders not to fall in love too early with the product or technology at the expense of being realistic and open. Otherwise, they are likely to build a very nice technology-driven product/service that nobody wants.

- Globalizing too early without having a clear product-market fit: Startups are sometimes tempted to expand overseas to increase market penetration, especially when the home market is not large enough. However, if the expansion is done too quickly without being sure that the product-market fit has been found, it can be distracting. Globalizing the operation adds complexity. It should be done when the product/service is stable and not evolving all the time because of new insights. The timing for globalization should be thought about carefully.

- Scaling too early: This is related to the point above. Scaling too early, when the company does not have yet the human resources or the financing necessary to scale, can result in the company spreading too thin on too many fronts. It often happens after the company raises a round of financing. The company has cash and spends it on the wrong things. By the time the organization realizes that spending isn't getting the company anywhere, it is often too late.

- Not paying for expertise: In some ways, this can be related to underspending. For example, finding an expert who knows what to do is not cheap. Many startups want to save money on the wrong thing. A VP of sales who knows what to do and whom to contact to increase traction is invaluable for a startup that has already achieved product–market fit. Paying for the right expertise at the right time is one of the difficult decisions that a startup needs to make to grow the company and be successful.

- Not listening to customers, ignoring data, or lacking evidence: One of the common mistakes young startups make is developing a product without enough input from customers. It is good to execute your vision; however, engaging with potential customers early on provides you the necessary proof that you are on the right path. You need to be able to gather evidence that you are solving a real problem. The data can be used to demonstrate that your idea is progressing and to create milestones. It may also tell you that you are on the wrong path and you need to pivot. The danger is to fall in love with your original idea without data backing it up and then not recognizing that it is failing. Do not go with your gut; go on evidence.

- Underestimating the length of the sales cycle and the cost of customer acquisition: Many startups are very optimistic that they can sell. However, the reality is that sales take time. For example, in a B2B business, building credibility and trust and creating partnerships can be a very long process. If your business does not account for this, you are in trouble. Often multiple levels of approvals are needed before completing a sale. Being able to estimate the time it takes to acquire customers is essential to understand how fast you can grow, to know how much cash you need, and to create realistic milestones. Many startups run out of money because they have been too aggressive in estimating sales timelines. Closely tracking how much it will cost you to acquire customers is also an important parameter as it will provide you indications on how viable your business model is and if you need to bring this cost down to be able to scale.

- Fearing failure: For a startup, the focus should be on learning quickly and adapting to the ever-changing conditions. We all make mistakes. However, the key is to make smart mistakes and to be resilient after mistakes to increase your chances of success. Being indecisive, a lack of confidence in your ability and the unique value in your product/service or showing a weak commitment do not align well with the needed traits of a founder who wants to succeed. In the end, a startup has to deal with uncertainty and chaos. It is the belief in the business, constantly making sacrifices, putting in the necessary time and facing challenges head-on that will pave the path toward success.

- Sacrificing simplicity and waiting too long to launch: Young founders tend to complicate things too much, from structuring partnership agreements to adding too many features to the product. Sometimes, the fear of doing things that they do not have experience with leads them to add complexity and to act on the cautious side at the expense of speed and productivity. Another mistake is waiting too long to release the product because founders want to add new capabilities. It is the objective of the MVP. Prioritizing speed with the smallest product that will help to alleviate the pain of their customers and lead them to buy is what startups want. Determining the functionalities which aren't crucial to the initial success is not always an easy thing to do for an early-stage startup.

- Hiring poorly and hiring too fast: At a small company, employees need to wear many hats, and they need to be prepared to wear many hats. Managing these expectations when hiring is important. In a growth stage, the startup needs to hire fast to maintain momentum and speed. Finding suitable people who fit with the company culture is not easy, especially in places like Silicon Valley, where there is much competition for talent. Hiring the wrong people could be devastating for an early-stage startup, as first hires have a critical influence on startup performance. Feeling pressure to hire quickly while the suitability of candidates is in doubt can also be devastating. Striking a balance between the speed of hiring and the suitability of the candidates available is another challenge that early-stage startups face. Filling the gaps via trusted partners and consultants can be one way to ease this challenge.

- Assuming virality: Startups evolving into the B2C space often assume that they will build the product/service, launch it, and then it will become viral. Services do not spontaneously go viral. Virality is the exception. A startup needs to spend some time thinking about how and why people are going to discover their offering.

- Getting distracted by feedback: Especially in the early phase, many people will offer feedback. It may be difficult to know the difference between what is important and what is not. In the end, the founders need to listen carefully and be guided by their vision and beliefs. It is their compass. People will give feedback based on their experience, knowledge, and expertise. However, it is the jobs of the founders to sort it out and to apply it to their startup without losing sight of what they want to achieve and of their vision. Nobody will do that for them.

- Not having the right co-founder: So many startups fail because of disagreements between co-founders. It is important for the co-founders to have known each other for a long time and to have had various types of experiences together to minimize potential issues later on. Building a startup is stressful and, eventually, under pressure, co-founders' flaws and weak points are exposed. Some mistakes are reversible, while some others, together with the unique characteristics of the other co-founder, are fatal. Assessing co-founders thoroughly before beginning the startup adventure is essential. While co-founders often bring you complementary skills, they can also be a source of friction down the line.

- Not maintaining relationships: Maintaining and nurturing relationships (e.g., with investors) is important as it is a source of knowledge, wisdom, and expertise for an early-stage startup. Every startup should have a close circle of trusted advisors who can provide an outside and unbiased view and help at critical moments. It takes time to build relationships and making sure that you have sufficient communication with your inner circle can make a difference. It is also important to be consistent, set a schedule, and stick to it. Another reason why harmony with investors matters is that when things go bad with an investor, it can get ugly pretty quickly.

The points above constitute some of the main pitfalls to avoid or at least to be aware of and useful tips which can significantly improve your chance of success. Each startup path is unique, and this list is by no means exhaustive but keeping it in mind will allow founders to build on top of many painful learnings and experiences that have been accumulated by their peers before them.

## 1.8. IN THE END, THE SUCCESS IS BEYOND YOUR CONTROL

It is somehow counterintuitive, but even with the most exceptional talent, the best effort, and much money, startups still manage to fail. Vinod Khosla, a Venture Capitalist (VC), co-founder of Sun Microsystems, and the founder of Khosla Ventures once said, "In my decades of encouraging entrepreneurs and innovation, I have learned that an entrepreneur probably only controls approximately 30 to 40%

of the factors that affect their success. Competitors and environmental circumstances often make up the rest" (Khosla, 2014). Some things are under the founder circle of influence (e.g., burn rate, whom you hire, product features) and others are not (e.g., competitors, economy, personal situations). It does not help to worry about things that you cannot control, though it is essential to understand the risks linked to uncontrollable factors. Founders should put all their energy into what they can directly impact without wasting energy on things that lie outside their circle of influence.

Because a startup cannot control everything, it needs to be prepared for worst-case scenarios, even if the worst-case scenario has a low probability of happening. Are you prepared if things do not work the way you thought? What about if incumbents are coming up with a solution competing with yours? A startup must imagine how they would handle unexpected situations as it can help to channel energy proactively toward activities, which may even reduce the likelihood of this to happen. For example, staying on top of the latest news and trends can help your new startup keep pace with the competition.

Another essential element contributing to startup success is timing. Timing cannot be consciously improved. If you have ever timed to create success, you know how hard it is to do so. Startup success depends on being in the right place at the right time. When economic times are good, the startup should run as fast as possible to build momentum and traction for the downtimes, and when times are not favorable, it is generally a good idea to defer all investments that are not necessary.

A startup should never get "comfortable" with its success. It is always good to have a sense of urgency and "controlled paranoia," pushing all your activities to new heights to prepare for the unexpected and to keep a clear focus on continued and accelerated growth. Taking the unknown, embracing it and focusing proactively on the things that you can control while acknowledging that there will always be factors beyond your control, is a recipe for success.

# CHAPTER 2

## The Innovation Roadmap

### 2.1. THE THREE STAGES OF A STARTUP

Innovation is characterized by uncertainty, risk, and difficult challenges which vary over time. It is happening in stages which have unique requirements. As shown in *Figure 2.1* below, every startup goes through three consecutive phases:

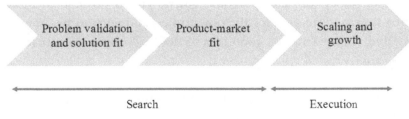

*Figure 2.1: The three stages of a startup constituting the innovation roadmap.*

- The first phase is validating with potential customers that the problem that they want to solve is a real problem their potential customers have and that there is a solution to it.

Interviews, rapid prototyping, and quick iterations are some of the modern methods used.

- The second phase is about validating that people are willing to pay for what you built or will build. Many startups fail not because their product does not do what it is supposed to do, but instead because they created something that people do not want. Startups must find the product-market fit.

- The third phase is about growth and scale to quickly accelerate the market traction after finding the product-market fit. This phase is about execution, building up resources and processes, and potentially reconsidering the channels to market to stimulate growth and create a sustainable business.

The first phase is very similar for corporations and startups. The main difference is that a startup often starts with the vision of the founder about the challenge he/she wants to tackle while the corporation often generates many ideas and sorts through them, considering the corporation strategic directions.

During the second phase, both startups and large corporations often follow the same process by talking to potential customers and through rapid iterations validating their hypotheses. It can be harder for corporations to determine the customer willingness to pay as large corporations are not always willing to put their brand on the line to experiment with the market. Some large companies use blind testing to evaluate new product ideas and protect their brand.

It is mainly with the third phase that there is a big difference between startups and large corporations. While large corporations execute with well-established processes, startups have to put operational procedures in place while progressing in the execution phase. It is a very challenging time for startups, as they are often not prepared to do so in terms of personnel, know-how, and support structure. On the other hand, for this third phase, large corporations tend to apply known processes which they have developed in the context of previous businesses, and it may not always be appropriate to the new opportunity that they are trying to create. While startups are bold and have to take risks, large corporations try to minimize the risks based on the knowledge that they already acquired from the creation of previous businesses. Using prior experience and processes may not always be suitable when facing new challenges, which sometimes require a new approach to achieve market success. For both startups and corporations, it is when the right people come together with the proper processes that they can execute effectively.

## 2.2. ZERO-IN ON THE PROBLEM TO SOLVE AND THE IMPORTANCE OF FOCUSING ON ISSUES YOU ARE HAVING

As a startup, you do not want to address just any problem. You want to solve the problem that is at the center of the customer pain or inconvenience. This problem sits at the heart of what your customer is trying to accomplish. You may have developed an excellent product, but if it is not functional or necessary for most of the people you are targeting, the chances that it will be widely adopted are very slim. When building a product, considering the user experience very carefully is essential. For example, Google Glass, while being a very well-designed product, failed to address what consumers wanted as many consumers found that the glasses were awkward to wear in public and not comfortable (Gibbs, 2014).

One of the keys to zero-in on the problem to solve is to ensure that you are digging deep enough to create something essential for users and not a mere optional capability that your customers don't care enough about to purchase your solution. I often hear the questions:

- How do you select the idea to pursue?
- How do you know that you identified a problem worth solving and can create a viable business by providing a solution for it?

This is the goal of the first phase of the innovation roadmap. You may have an insight into what your customers are trying to accomplish and the problems that they face or the workarounds they use. You may also have a solution which is faster, easier to use, more effective than current solutions, or just more affordable. You validate it via a deep understanding of your potential customers and their goals along with rapid experiments allowing you to gather evidence and confidence that you are on the right path. By understanding the workflow of your potential customers and what they are trying to accomplish, you can narrow the product focus.

During the startup early stages, the founder should always figure out the answers to the following questions:

- What does the user need and want?
- How much would the user be willing to pay for our solution, and how can we validate it?
- Why is our solution better than what exists and why would the user change the way he/she has been doing the task at hand?
- What would prompt a user not to accept our solution?
- What are other possible alternatives the user could adopt?
- What is frustrating the user, and is there a deeper problem than the one my solution is currently solving?

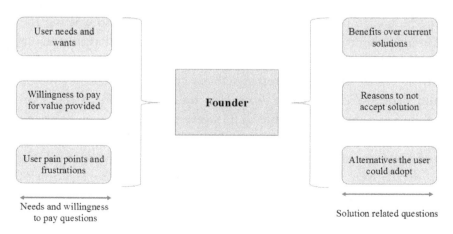

*Figure 2.2: Important questions a founder should answer.*

These questions, clustered in *Figure 2.2* in two groups related to the user needs/willingness to pay and the solution itself, will allow your startup to identify critical problems and build a unique solution that addresses a fundamental issue that has not yet been solved by the competition.

Remember, it is worth taking the time and effort to confirm that you are solving an essential problem so that you can create a genuinely useful and competitive solution. It is the beginning of the startup adventure, and what follows depends on how thorough you have been in identifying evidence that this is the right thing to do. A startup cannot afford to solve the wrong problem as it will lead to an unsuccessful journey or a lot of time and resources wasted. To gather evidence, it is essential to:

- Interview potential customers and have them talk about what they are trying to accomplish and how they have been doing it.
- Get feedback with early prototypes.
- Understand the competition and alternative solutions in the market.

One way to deeply understand potential users is to tackle real-world problems that you are experiencing. There are three things that the best startup ideas have in common: 1) they are something the founders themselves want, 2) they focus on solutions that the startup can build, 3) they concentrate on problems and solutions that few others realize are worth creating. Many companies, such as Google and Facebook, began this way. It is indeed possible to focus on solving someone else's problems. However, in doing so, you lose the advantage of being your customer. It is easier to realize inefficiencies and inconveniences when it is your problem. Finally, as we will talk in details later in this book, one of the keys is in the execution of ideas. Ideas are worth nothing unless you are an effective executor that can implement that idea.

## 2.3. THE POWER OF AN AMBITIOUS VISION AND SOLVING BIG PROBLEMS

In February 2018, CB Insights analyzed more than 100 startup post-mortems and reported that the number one reason startups fail was not about running out of cash but instead because they did not tackle a big enough problem (CB_Insights, 2018). They failed because they were not tackling issues that were interesting to solve and served a market need. Besides addressing a real need, a startup who wants to make it big should tackle big problems. There are several reasons for this:

- If you do not want to face competition, you need to build a novel solution. Focusing on a big problem enhances your chances in doing this.
- By providing a solution to important issues, your startup will not be at the mercy of fleeting trends as your customers will need to purchase from you for years to come.
- You are more likely to get in front of big-name customers.

When building your startup, it may seem attractive to work on an idea you already know where to start on. However, if the problem can be so intuitively solved, the chances that somebody else previously thought about it is very likely. For considerable challenges, it is much less evident as it is hard to solve big problems. Creating the next mobile application to find a suitable restaurant is likely to be less sustainable than a medical imaging solution allowing doctors to diagnose cancer earlier. If there is no real pain, there is no actual pain point! If you've got to convince other people the problem you are solving exists, you have got an issue. If, on the other hand, you have tried to find a solution for the challenge you are trying to solve and have been struggling because the answer is not apparent, you may be on the right track.

Another trend is that building a business to be successful and make money is no longer enough. It must also have a positive impact on society. The key is how to make your vision to impact society profitable. While everybody wants to make money, most people would rather do something meaningful for them and fun, and do something that matters. Creating a new business is hard, and if you are going to start a business, start an incredibly ambitious one: Solve a problem that is as hard as your skill set allows.

While everybody understands it is difficult to change the world as it requires breakthrough technologies and significant investment, setting up an ambitious target and changing the world one step at a time is one way to improve how people live while keeping an eye on the big picture. Peter Diamandis from Singularity University has said: "Want to be a Billionaire? Solve a Billion-Person Problem" (Winfrey, 2014). Improving people's lives is the best way to build a sustainable business. Facebook started by exploiting our human need for connecting with friends. They created the "newsfeed" to keep us occupied with a stream of comments, photos, and shared information. This was the first step toward providing a sense of connection to others. These examples show that an ambitious vision with a step by step execution that provides value at each step is a recipe for success.

## 2.4. DISCOVERING WHO YOUR CUSTOMER IS

Traditional customer research focuses on demographics, including age, gender, location, and/or income. While these are important, it is vital to understand the factors that lie beneath the surface. What are their interests, passions, skills, beliefs, and values? Having an in-depth knowledge of who the startup customers are, is probably the only way for a startup to be successful. At the beginning of the startup life, it is all about feedback. You need a few people to try out your prototypes and let you know what works for them and what doesn't. The people you know who love to try new things and share their opinions are good candidates. These first people can be called "early adopters" (potential ones at this stage), and they are the people the startup needs at the beginning. You may have plans to offer many features or services, but initially focusing on providing too many capabilities results only in more confusion. It is essential to prioritize what you need to test and what kind of feedback you want to collect. The critical hypotheses should be tested first because, if they are not valid, you will need to pivot. Initially, you may not be able to predict what the result will be, but it is often great to follow your gut feeling. During this phase, it will be essential to observe, listen, interpret, and involve your potential customers deeply. Personas—fictional characters representing different user types that might benefit from your solution—are often used to understand customer needs.

The feedback that you will get with potential early adopters will provide you insights into what kind of customers you are targeting. At some point, you will have to ask people to buy your product. It is a critical step as until a person is buying your product, he/she is not your customer. It is when people are buying your product that you can validate you have the right product for them. The difference between success and failure is often as simple as asking them to buy your product.

During this customer discovery phase, it is essential to test and validate your hypotheses about the following topics (also summarized in *Figure 2.3*):

- Are you solving a real problem?
- Is your solution attractive for your potential customers, and what are the critical and minimum set of features that will be just enough to satisfy early customers, often commonly referred to as the Minimum Viable Product (MVP)?
- How much are your potential customers willing to pay?
- How will you go to the market and let your customers know that you exist?

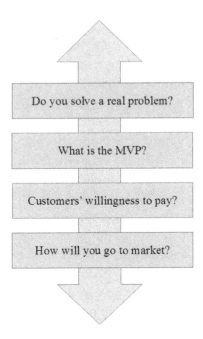

*Figure 2.3: Important hypotheses to be tested and validated.*

Finding out who your customers are should be an iterative process, for which each cycle lasts at most a few weeks. Based on the initial feedback, you should refine the hypotheses and repeat the cycle. As you better understand your customers, it is essential to dive into the details of how to set up your business to serve them best.

Many startups have offerings that interest different customers. However, because startups have limited resources, each company needs to prioritize which customer segments to target. Understanding your customer segments helps zero-in on the most specific customer problems to address. The key is to narrow the characteristics of the prototypical customer. Initially, the goal is to define early adopters/ customer segments, not necessarily a mainstream customer.

## 2.5.  COMING UP WITH THE SOLUTION AND VALIDATING IT

Startups, at least initially, have to be very careful with their limited cash resources. Many entrepreneurs get stuck in the beginning, often when they have an engineering background, because they think that the first thing you need to do is to build a solution and to demonstrate it as a step toward a scalable and robust version of the product. However, initially, the goal is mainly to validate the hypotheses, especially the critical ones, without necessarily building a solution. Developing a product should be done after defining a solution and identifying the MVP.

Identifying and validating the solution can be quite inexpensive. It can take the form of mockups, quick prototypes assembled using available parts, soliciting interest via ads, collecting E-mails via a launch page, or videos. At the initial stage, it is essential not to fall in love with the solution but instead to focus on understanding the problem deeply. It will be the basis for understanding the solution specifications. Concentrating on developing the solution too early often leads to a waste of resources as requirements are still fuzzy, and a more thorough understanding of the customer is needed. As shown in *Figure 2.4*, it is also important not to get stuck in the experimental phase but use experiments to learn and to make progress that will lead to innovation.

*Figure 2.4: Innovation is about making progress via experiments.*

Validating your idea and coming up with the solution needed to solve the problem that you are seeing is often about asking the right questions. Interviewing potential customers is a way to do this. Instead of asking questions about solution development, entrepreneurs should first ask whether they should develop it. In other words, is their solution the right fit for the problem they are trying to solve? Some possible validation results of your idea and the proposed solution could come from obtaining pre-orders for the initial version of the product.

At the core, validation is about experimentation. You make assumptions, you test, and, based on the results, you develop new ones. Experimenting allows you to either prove or disprove your assumptions—or test your hypotheses. For startups, validation is an essential activity. Founders should look to incorporate validation processes into every phase of a startup's life cycle. Validation helps in avoiding costly and time-consuming mistakes.

## 2.6. FOCUSING ON SPEED, QUICK LEARNING, AND ITERATIONS

When I was in charge of innovation at Panasonic in Silicon Valley, my tagline was: "Speed is more important than being 100% right." The main focus should be on speed. However, the focus of large corporations is often to minimize risks and to move when they are confident they are in the right direction. The problem is that when they achieve certainty, it is often too late. Startups have an advantage as compared to large corporations. If they spend too much time trying to get everything perfect, they run out of money. While in many situations a lack of resources is a disadvantage, it is the sense of urgency that pushes the startup to innovate quickly and to develop new approaches to overcome the uncertainty coming with the creation of a new venture. For some inexperienced entrepreneurs, perfection can be the enemy of speed, and sometimes it can delay their market launch.

To build a startup, you need to be agile and quick. Slow and steady progress is not enough to succeed. A startup has to be ready to learn, adapt, and quickly change direction if necessary. It is life in the fast lane. For some inexperienced entrepreneurs, it can be challenging and sometimes scary. In a large corporation, the traditional business process is about planning. It requires time and money that startups do not have, at least initially. Instead of relying on a rigid concrete plan, startups implement an *agile process* and a quick feedback loop, as illustrated in *Figure 2.5*. They learn on the go based on experiments and assumption validation. Since learning is happening in real-time, even if something unexpected comes up, the startup can adapt and still move forward. Corporations' fear of mistakes leads to failure and delays, while startups allow themselves to make mistakes, to learn, to iterate and test small aspects of the product. The bias is toward action instead of overthinking every step along the way. Successful startups know that every feature does not have to be ready from the beginning. They do not overbuild. When building a startup, the secret to success is speed. The quicker you can prove your concept, the faster you can make money and learn about the market to grow your company. The can-do attitude and open communication that characterize the first few iterations produce magic.

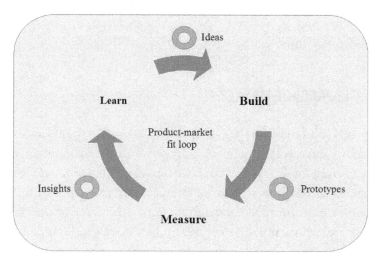

*Figure 2.5: The quick feedback loop.*

While large corporations measure success in terms of "Return on Investment" (ROI), startups measure success, at least initially, in terms of speed of progress/learning. For a startup, the following steps are practical:

- Start with potentially the most significant wins that can be realized quickly and make sure that you have resources to process them.

31

- Learn from your previous iterations to increase the success rate.
- Avoid discussions on long-term planning. For a startup, a year is already a long time.
- Think twice before starting big projects, as they are usually riskier and more time-consuming given the limited resources that a startup has.

For large corporations, one way to accelerate the pace of innovation and new business creation is to target collaborations using open innovation (Chesbrough, 2003) (Chesbrough, 2006) (Chesbrough, 2011). When implemented successfully, open innovation can result in win-win arrangements and increase speed to market. For startups, the main benefit is usually to leverage the resources and go-to-market channels of large corporations. However, as startups move toward launch, they may be slowed down by the bureaucracy, such as legal and IP negotiations, that a large company requires.

## 2.7. THE PRODUCT-MARKET FIT

The product-market fit (Ries, 2011) is a critical step toward the success of a startup or any new business venture. It requires a strong understanding of the needs and the market that you are serving. Success lies at the intersection of the product you are building, the audience or customers who care about your product, and the business model required to entice a customer to buy your product. Achieving a product-market fit often necessitates many iterations and fine-tuning as obtaining a fit between the three parameters above requires experiments and insights acquired over time. The market is often leading the search. If a large market does not exist, even with a great product, it will be challenging to build a sustainable business. Depending on who is looking at your new business venture, they may emphasize some aspects more than others. For example, in some cases, investors may weigh the marketplace more than people, as the team can be enhanced or shaped if the opportunity is present.

While the product-market fit is an objective, it is not often clear how to reach it as you usually know when you get there, but it can be challenging to specify it. Entrepreneurs have to define value hypotheses and test them to see if these hypotheses are valid or not. A value hypothesis indicates the fundamental assumptions about why a customer is likely to buy your product. Startups and founders often stumble on the product-market fit. For many startups, serendipity plays a significant role. However, the process to achieve product-market fit is now well known, as shown in the next chapter. The value hypothesis defines the "*what,*" the "*who*" and the "*how*" of the business that you are trying to create. Many iterations may be needed to test the value hypothesis. Iterations can involve the problem itself, the business model, the type of customer targeted, or any combinations of those. They answer the following questions: "What are you going to build, who are the customers who have the pain you are solving, are they willing to pay for it, and what is the business model you are going to use to deliver it?"

Finding the product-market fit is like finding resonance with your customers and getting on the same wavelength with them about the relevance to them of the problem that you are solving and the solution that you are bringing forward. As illustrated in *Figure 2.6,* it is like fitting two pieces of a puzzle inside the business world. Finding the product-market fit shows that you are creating value for your customers, and this will enable growth for your business. Initially, for a startup, it is the only thing that matters. It is also essential to understand that product-market fit is not a one-time thing. Your product, customers, and the market continually evolve. So, you should always wonder and question if your product-market fit is still valid or if you need to make some adjustments. Startups should do whatever is required to get to the product-market fit, including listening carefully to their target customers, moving to a different market, modifying their product, or modifying their business model. It is achieved by talking to potential customers and getting them involved and engaged in your search for the product-market fit. Usually, at the beginning stage of a startup, this is everyone's job, not only the founder. Most startups fail because they cannot reach the product-market fit or because they think they did and go into scaling mode too early.

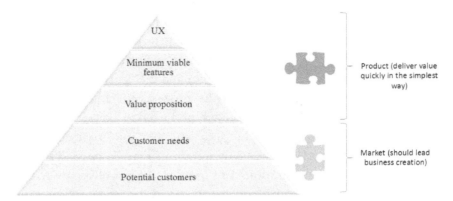

*Figure 2.6: An illustration of the product-market fit.*

To test the product-market fit, you need to gather enough evidence. The opinion of one customer is not enough. It is just an opinion. You should collect data over and over again from many potential customers before jumping to conclusions. Having some traction is also not enough to conclude that you have a product-market fit as you may have only reached early adopters and your cost of customer acquisition could be too high to have a business that can scale. It is also essential to focus on one vertical at a time instead of diluting resources toward all the possible markets. After you reach the product-market fit for the first vertical chosen—often because it is the quickest way to go to market—you can decide to address other tangential verticals as you do not want to make the same mistakes twice and startups have limited resources. Furthermore, the go-to-market strategy, sales cycle, or how you sell may be different from vertical to vertical. If you do not have customers lining up for your products or your offering is not sticky enough, you should go back to the drawing board and rethink about product and market strategy.

## 2.8. HOW DO YOU KNOW THAT YOU HAVE A PRODUCT-MARKET FIT?

A question often raised by founders or investors is, "How do we know that we have a product-market fit?" The answer to this question is you can always feel that you reached it. When suddenly, your customers are buying the products faster than you can make them, they become your salespeople, they share positive experiences, and the value of your product spreads quickly by word of mouth. Conversely, when you are not there yet, your early customers are not getting enough value out of your product, you are not acquiring customers fast enough, sales cycles are too long, many deals do not close, and many reviews are negative. If this happens, it is time to revisit your product-market fit before going further as your product is not satisfying the market.

Some more objective measures indicate some amount of product-market fit, such as the Net Promoter Score (NPS) (Reichheld, 2003) which is based on a simple survey asking customers how likely they are to recommend your product on a scale from one to ten. The NPS is an excellent tool to predict the magnitude of customer love and satisfaction for your solution. Churn and user retention are other measures. Looking at how many customers stop using your solution and how long they use your product before leaving is an indication of the value that you are providing to your customers and how sticky is your product.

For an entrepreneur, it is essential to use some of these measures as roughly 70% of the startups fail because they are scaling prematurely without having reached the product-market fit. Startups tend to underestimate the time that it takes to come up with a product-market fit and as a result, based on some preliminary traction that often comes from early adopters, feel pressure to try scaling earlier than they should. For example, hiring a full sales force too fast, or globalizing the operation too early leads the company to burn through cash and fail to meet revenue expectations. Getting some traction with a product which is not right for the market can become a disadvantage as it can hide all sorts of problems that can hinder the growth of the company.

## 2.9. DEVELOPING THE VALUE PROPOSITION AND FINDING THE RIGHT MARKET CHANNELS BEFORE SCALING AND GROWING

While working on the product-market fit, startups must connect their offering with the customer needs in a clear and focused way so that it can instantly resonate with customers. As learning happens and insights are continuously acquired, the value proposition is tuned and positioned as compared to competitors in your market to motivate customers to buy your products. The value proposition (Osterwalder, Pigneur, Bernarda, & Smith, 2014) is also sometimes synonymous with unique selling proposition. It should include critical insights you learned from your customers along with your product strengths as compared to other offerings in the market.

It is essential to develop a crisp and concise value proposition as it forces startups to focus on what is significant. It also enables the company to stand out immediately when compared to the competition while also providing clear directions for the company itself. Below is an example of a value proposition or positioning:

> *"A platform and ecosystem for seniors and caregivers to build communities and a network of care with a fully integrated communication system."*

This value proposition emphasizes the company positioning for its targeted population. In the particular case above, it is about building communities and a network of care for seniors and caregivers focusing on communication. Depending on your customer segments, it is sometimes useful to have several variants of the value proposition, which emphasizes the particular needs of specific audiences or verticals.

Testing the value proposition in the field is crucial. However, initially, you may not have everything needed to demonstrate it. The best way to approach it initially is often to fake the value proposition in the most credible way and test it. It is a practice that Alberto Savoia called "pretotyping" (Savoia, 2019). He defined pretotyping as "fake it and test it before you make it."

After establishing the value proposition and validating a product-market fit, critical considerations for startups are to identify the right channels to sell or distribute products. To identify these channels, you need to understand how you need to sell your product (e.g., with or without installation, bundle with another product) and how customers will know about it and will buy it (e.g., online, via traditional retailers or partners). When you are trying to find the right channels for your business, it is also essential to understand what are the costs involved (Moore, 2014). For example:

- What are the channel costs, direct and indirect? Will these costs cut into your margin?
- How effective will the channel be to reach out to your customers?
- What will be your cost of customer acquisition after you include all the charges?

There are many different types of customer acquisition channels (Weinberg & Mares, 2015). They depend on the product or service and the markets targeted (e.g., B2B or B2C). The most common ones include:

- Advertisement.
- Referrals and word of mouth (for a viral product).
- Landing pages, articles, and Search Engine Optimization (SEO).
- Direct sales.
- Partnerships.

While the above list is not exhaustive, these channels are often the selected ones. Each startup needs to investigate the right ones for its business. Content marketing, social media marketing, E-mail campaigns, or trade shows are some other ways to reach out to potential customers. A startup should experiment with traditional channels but also some new ones that have a substantial alignment with their market, and are not traditional. When testing channels, it is essential to track your customer acquisition channels and to be methodical as this will give you some insights into what is working and what is not. It will allow you to find the most effective channels. In the end, you are looking for the channels that provide you the cheapest cost of customer acquisition and are the most successful at attracting your customers. You should also keep in mind that at different times in the life of your business, some channels may be more suitable than others depending on what you want to optimize for (e.g., cost, learning, volume). Each marketing channel is different and unique, and it is vital to select channels that work for you and fit with your desired target audience.

## 2.10. SCALING AND ACCELERATING GROWTH

Being able to quickly multiply success for a beachhead market that you got into initially is not the same as building for sustainable growth. At the beginning stage of a startup, the focus should be on the short term and priorities. As the startup grows, it is crucial to create a real market identity and to create a strategy to build capacity that will allow the startup to scale (Moore, 2014). For sustainable growth, it is vital to design an organization that can scale. Scaling up to manage growth involves looking forward and asking yourself what the organization should look like to support your expansion, considering the competitive landscape and the threats that your business faces.

Scaling involves standardization, cohesive processes, and defining repeatable approaches. While it should not sacrifice freedom and creativity, the primary purpose of standards and carefully designed workflows is to avoid losing time and energy on repetitive tasks. A critical aspect of scaling is automation. It takes some time at the front-end, but as you are expanding it pays in the long term. It can also be critical to outsource the non-essential roles or activities and to focus on your core competencies.

Part of the scaling process is to establish your "business roadmap" and the timeline associated with it. Having a clear picture of where the company will be three or five years down the road helps to create a strategy and make decisions that fall into this strategy. It also helps to set a "North Star" and the communication with the internal team. It should go in parallel with a plan which will allow you to finance the expansion of your business and a cash flow analysis to make sure that you will not run out of money executing your plan. It should also include a marketing strategy to make sure you reach out to enough customers so that your expansion is realistic.

One element which is crucial but sometimes overlooked is hiring. Having the right people in place will allow you to delegate so that "operating" the expansion can be taken care of while you concentrate on other tasks. One way to do this is to hire people with the right skill sets and mindsets. It is not easy and can take time. Trade-off decisions on direct hires versus contracted/outsourced capabilities are often required to capture the necessary expertise. Experience shows that if there is not enough emphasis on HR to hire the people right for the job, the expansion is likely to run into problems that can have serious consequences. When employing people who are just OK for the job, they will probably become subpar when the company grows and therefore, become a problem. Legal help is also not optional. As the company grows, not having a general counsel to explain to the CEO what is legally possible and where the limits are is problematic. Typically, these capabilities need to be put in place when the company grows over 50 to 100 people as when the company reaches more than 50 people, the communication between management and employees starts to become more difficult. It is then a good time to start layering additional capabilities such as HR and legal.

You may decide that the best way is to expand internationally to scale your new venture. As mentioned earlier, before doing so, it is imperative to be confident that you have a robust product-market fit as the added complexity linked to an international expansion can be detrimental to your startup. Another consideration is to prioritize the markets where you want to expand. Many startups see the United States as one of the most attractive markets. However, it is essential to keep in mind that the United States has different regulations for each state, which can potentially complicate your expansion. Independently of the market you are considering to expand into, you should ask yourself the following questions:

- Is the market large enough?
- How does this market fit into my overall strategy?
- Is the market growing for my product?
- How well will my product sell in the market, and does it need to be localized?
- How can I validate the product-market fit for this new market?
- What does the competition look like, and can I win the market?
- Which channels can I use in this new market? Do I need to partner?
- How much investment do I need to start in this new market?
- Can I capture enough share of this new market?
- Do I have the human resources to tackle this new market? If not, how will I bring them onboard?
- What is the impact of time zone differences in the way I will be operating, and how will I communicate?
- Are there any synergies between this new market and the ones I am already serving?

By answering these questions, you will be in a position to make the best decision. You should also spend time in this new market so that you can make your opinion based on what you learn and experience, as in the end it will be up to you to decide. As markets keep changing, it is a good practice to continually re-evaluate if the decision still makes sense according to the results obtained and the state of the company.

The above points need to be addressed to be able to scale and grow. Another essential element is a mindset enabling to think big and remove limitations. These two growth mindset characteristics are required to succeed. A founder needs to take all the appropriate risks to win over the competition and become #1 in the market(s) targeted. Winning the market should be the goal. Founders are often learning on the go to do this. Quick learning and adaptability are characteristics of successful founders.

While the company focuses on winning the market, it is also essential to think about the next product and to keep innovating. The competition is not standing still, and if competitors come up with a better product, they will displace you. So, while growing and scaling it is also critical to invest in the future and to have a roadmap for new capabilities. During the innovation process, creating the barriers to entry to make sure that the business is sustainable should also be part of the strategy. Examples of barriers to entry are granted patents, resources (e.g., data) not available to competitors, or access to exclusive distribution channels.

Finally, when scaling, many companies evolve from a product-centric model to a distribution-centric model as a distribution-centric model allows them to reach their customers faster and more widely. It is undoubtedly the case for a B2B offering. Initially, founders spend much time on the problem, developing the solution, and finding the product-market fit. It is vital to understand that the product is different from the business and that focusing on competitive advantages such as the business model, the relation between price and value, and distribution channels should be essential areas of focus and possible business differentiations as the company scales.

# CHAPTER 3

## Iterative and Evidence-Based Approaches

### 3.1. FROM TECHNOLOGY BREAKTHROUGHS TO DESIGN-BASED APPROACHES

When considering innovation, for many years, it has been natural to think about technology. In the last decades, advances in areas such as wireless communication, HD-TV, blockchain technology (Norman, 2017), speech recognition (Junqua & Haton, 1996) (Junqua, 2000), and machine learning (Bengio, 2009) created many radical innovations and transformed our daily lives. These breakthrough technologies took years to develop but ultimately changed our world.

Social changes generally go along with advances in technology as a consequence of changing economies and ways of carrying out life's various activities. For example, the era of digital transformation brought new ways of organizing information and integrating it. However, with the ever-accelerating pace of change and the introduction of new products, a purely technocentric view of innovation is less and less sustainable.

Another way to innovate is via market-driven research, though we know that when you ask people what they want or what they need, they usually cannot answer or have a very narrow view based on their experiences. They tend to respond based on what they know. So, this approach leads most of the time to evolutionary innovation. To keep up with our very fast-changing world, the evolution of society and the need for both incremental and radical innovation, it is evident that new innovative approaches are needed. As Tim Brown, CEO of the Design Firm IDEO, stated: "What we need are new choices, instead of continuously optimizing the existing ones." We need new ways of looking at the human condition and the global challenges that we are facing, such as health, poverty, or education. It is the area of design-driven innovation (Verganti, 2009), as shown in *Figure 3.1* below.

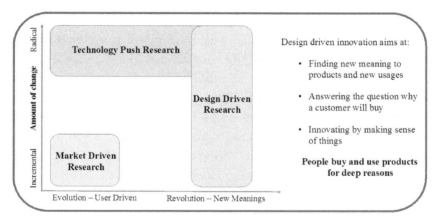

*Figure 3.1: The three innovation strategies.*

In the last decade, we have been witnessing the rise of design-driven innovation where the focus is not to push new technology but to discover new meaning. Design-driven innovation aims at finding new usages and new meanings for products (Brown, 2019). A very well-known example of making sense of things is the iPod where Apple came up with a different choice and meaning by offering people the ability to carry their music with them and creating new usage by listening to music on the go.

Design-driven innovation has become increasingly recognized and supported by a growing number of companies as a critical enabler for innovation and business success and as a vital source of competitive advantage (Liedtka & Ogilvie, 2011). Companies like Apple, Samsung, and others have shown in the context of many products how important it became. Design-driven organizations are embracing customer centricity and have put designing for their users at the heart of what they do. Design-driven innovation relies on the observation that the usefulness and desirability of a product are not determined by its technical capabilities but rather by how the experience it provides brings value to customers' lives. Instead of starting by focusing on technology, the idea of design innovation is to begin by identifying the issues/problems to solve. The methods used provide seeds and hints/insights which will guide the team toward the development of solutions addressing this understanding to provide user value. These solutions (often, in the early stage, via mockups or rough prototypes) are provided to potential customers to validate the hypotheses. This validation process that Steve Blank and Bob Dorf call "customer development" (Blank & Dorf, 2012) guides the team to identify the technologies and the MVP that the team will develop. With this model, technology is not a focus, but a means to create a solution for solving the problem identified. The emphasis on technology comes to light after the team knows very clearly which problem to solve and how to solve it.

For this model, rapid iterations and fast learning from users are essential to quickly understand if the hypotheses make sense and if the team is headed in the right direction. Instead of spending a lot of time planning or on market research, there is a bias for action, involving potential customers very early on to provide feedback about the early hypotheses and developments.

Design-driven innovation is a well-accepted approach in the United States as a modern way of creating a new business. It has been a little more challenging in Asia and Europe where there is still a strong focus on technology as the first step to create a new business that is generally followed by a market search for the developed technology.

## 3.2. THE POWER OF PROBLEM EXPLORATION

As the statement often attributed to Albert Einstein says: "If I had an hour to solve a problem, I would spend fifty-five minutes to think about the problem and five minutes thinking about solutions." This saying illustrates how the problem itself becomes the basis of the solution. A genuine understanding of the problem is the starting point for any creative solution, and it becomes the best resource for innovators.

Part of the challenge is that problem-finding is not necessarily obvious, and it comes to light from moments of insight or intuition, called "*aha*" moments in the design world. A new way of looking at the problem triggers the "*aha*" moment. This "reframing" or redefinition of the problem starts the search for solutions that can provide new value so that the solution solves the customer pain point discovered and is workable. Thinking out of the box and reframing the problem leads to new solutions while moving along the usual and traditional trajectory is likely to lead to incremental improvements. It is the power of new choices and problem redefinition.

To explore the problem space, it is generally essential to trust your gut feeling and to prototype to explore, instead of prototyping for developing a solution. Initial prototypes make initial ideas or assumptions available, and allow others to provide feedback, play with the prototype and understand the meaning of your hypothesis. It also offers fresh insights from people who may not be familiar with your problem or idea. It will lead to new perspectives about the problem or solution. Different ways to look at the problem and leveraging diversity help lead to novel solutions. The idea of problem exploration is about playing with possibilities ("*what if*") to create new "*aha*" moments that will give rise to radical innovation and solutions.

It is often helpful to have a space large enough to investigate. If you look at the problem that similar individuals have, you will likely see it the same way. However, if you look at extreme situations and extreme users, you are likely to understand more of the problem space. Extreme users are helpful to broaden your thoughts and help you think differently. It is also the case of extreme situations which often create the conditions for new insights and directions.

Defining a meaningful problem to solve, which has a viable market, is probably one of the most challenging parts of the creation of any new business venture. Both the design thinking (Plattner, Meinel, & Leifer, 2010) (Brown, 2019) and lean startup approaches (Blank & Dorf, 2012) that we will cover in the next sections provide a framework to synthesize your observations about your potential users and to come up with insights. These insights will be the basis of your unique value proposition.

## 3.3. DRIVING INNOVATION BY TALKING TO CUSTOMERS AND BEING CUSTOMER OBSESSED

Traditional market research used to be very popular to extract the next things that the product development team should start developing. However, this leads frequently to minor incremental improvement. Often people do not know what they need. If you want to drive innovation and new choices, you need to hear from your customers. Listening to your customers will allow you to extract the useful insights which will guide you toward your next innovation. It is why you need to make sure that there is a constant flow of communication about wishes, opinions, suggestions, difficulties, workarounds, or inconveniences flowing from your sales team to your product team. You need to tear down the wall between your customers and your product innovation team. *Figure 3.2* shows an innovation process driven by customer input.

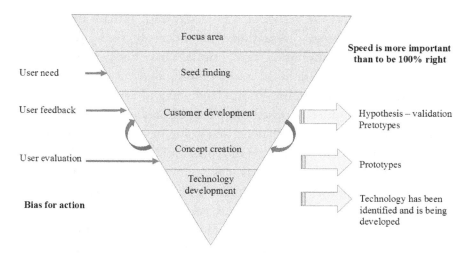

*Figure 3.2: Customer-driven innovation.*

To be able to get useful feedback from your customers, you need to be able to ask clear and straightforward questions aimed at understanding their pain points. Confusing or complicated questions will lead to confusing or fuzzy answers. With the responses that you get, you need to derive useful innovation directions. The customer feedback that you gather may not always be directly or immediately applicable to what you may need to do to innovate. However, it is generally a trigger that makes you realize, directly or indirectly, what your next steps will be.

In this new era of digital transformation, understanding your customers, not just knowing your customers, is a key to long-term success. It provides the basis for disruption and allows startups or forward-thinking brands to create disruption and fuel long-term growth with actionable insights. A common mistake of startup founders is to pay too little attention to customers and to prioritize creativity and technology as compared to making their customers happy and delivering superior user experience.

Some companies, such as Amazon, are said to be customer obsessed. Being customer obsessed goes beyond extracting the needs and wants of customers. It is the result of a proactive rather than a reactive approach to customer orientation. Customer-obsessed companies come up with innovations that their customers have not even imagined possible. They take as input the understanding of their customers and transform this understanding in fundamental and unexpected ways. To become a customer-obsessed company requires a company culture and mindset, a collective behavior, and going beyond knowing your customers, all in order to understand them and be successful. It needs strong leadership from the top as it is more about transforming the lives of your customers to offer them a better future. At Amazon, every innovation starts with a press release which articulates the value of a new product for their targeted customers. After there is an agreement on the customer value, the product team works backward from there.

Often people use the terms "customer orientation," "customer-centric," "experience design," or "customer obsession" in an interchangeable way. These terms are often overused and misused. As described earlier, customer obsession arises from a proactive mindset, and customer-obsessed companies go beyond the "needs and wants" of their customers. In this era of digital transformation—besides Amazon, who is leading the way—Apple, Airbnb, and Slack are some examples of companies doing a great job at understanding their customers.

## 3.4. ITERATIVE AND RAPID PROTOTYPING

Web companies made famous the notion of A/B testing and rapid iteration to test customer behavior. Since then, this idea has become a force in the business world, not only for Web-based development but also for software and hardware products. Products are now rolled out quickly to get customer feedback and incorporate it in the next iteration.

Rapid prototyping and iterative design are mainly used in the early stage of product development to test assumptions and validate critical hypotheses early on, based on customer feedback. It allows a very efficient validation process, minimizing development costs, accelerating time to market while reducing the risks of building something that is not accepted by the market. At the core, rapid prototyping and iterative methodologies are about learning and progressing to the next level. At every iteration, feedback is occurring, guiding the next iteration toward the right direction. During this process, the notion of "prototype" is sometimes misunderstood. A prototype is not an image of the final product/solution, but rather something that tests an assumption/hypothesis. It is a tool used to learn and validate rather than a product or solution adequately addressing the customer problem that needs to be solved.

This iterative mindset, illustrated in *Figure 3.3*, has been shown to drive some of the most successful companies in the world and it is often a characteristic of Silicon Valley, led by design firms like IDEO and Stanford University. This methodology has found its way from IT and manufacturing to marketing and business development. The figure below summarizes this methodology, which allows companies to make decisions based on evidence from customer feedback.

Iterative and rapid prototyping is a way to accelerate learning and to minimize the risks of going in the wrong direction. During this stage of the development process, open innovation (Chesbrough, 2003) can help as another source of knowledge and speed. During the product-market fit, and even at later stages, it is all about speed learning, and, depending on the expertise available internally, bringing up additional resources/knowledge can become handy. Open innovation is used more by innovation labs from large corporations than startups, as corporations have the monetary resources to do so at the early stage of an innovation project while startups are often not able to do so due to budget constraints.

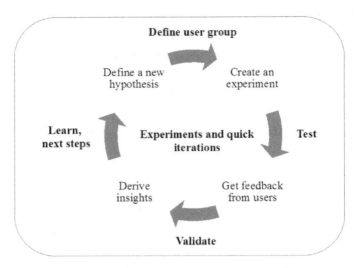

*Figure 3.3: The iterative experimentation loop.*

## 3.5.   A DIVERSE TEAM FOR INCREASED INNOVATION

There is ample evidence in the literature that diversity increases innovation and drives growth, but innovation teams do not always understand the meaning associated with diversity, what kinds of diverse experience are needed and for what purpose. At the early stage of a startup or an innovation team, diversity of expertise, culture, background, and experiences bring new perspectives contributing to different types of ideas and concepts. Building a team representing a broad sample of skills (e.g., hardware and software engineers, designers, experts in human factors, ethnographers) will provide different views and ideas about the problems to solve and technology trends leading to possible solutions. On the other end, including at some stage, a representative sample of the customer population (e.g., to obtain feedback) leads to understanding customers better and creating products that a broader cross-section of the society will use. We can distinguish two types of diversity: inherent and acquired. "Inherent diversity" involves the traits you are born with such as gender and ethnicity while "acquired diversity" includes traits that you gain from experiences such as cultural sensitivity and expertise.

Both are important to create an environment for generating and valuing out-of-the-box ideas.

While team diversity is essential, to boost innovation, it is also necessary for the company leaders to establish a culture in which employees across the board feel free to contribute ideas. Leaders who provide a way to consider diverse voices are more likely than others who don't to unleash value-driven insights. With a wide variety of contributors, a company is more likely to understand unmet needs than a company composed of people having similar inherent and acquired traits.

When companies want to have multiple points of view represented by a diverse group of employees, they generally look at various characteristics. These include demographic, discipline (e.g., software/ hardware engineer, designer), knowledge and education, domain and range of experience (e.g., generalist versus expert), extracurricular interest, team player or individual contributor. However, making sure that employees have shared values and fit in the company culture is also an essential element for building trust and harnessing the benefits that diversity can bring. It is a balance that the company's leadership must foster.

## 3.6. DESIGN THINKING

Design thinking (Plattner, Meinel, & Leifer, 2010) (Brown, 2019) is a customer-centric iterative process in which we seek to understand user needs based on assumptions and hypotheses aimed at identifying alternative novel strategies and solutions that may not be instantaneously obvious. Out of this process, design concepts aimed at providing new user value emerge. Design thinking is an iterative process which starts by observing users in their natural environment and developing empathy for these users.

The design thinking process identifies new needs or new user choices. Then, via rapid prototyping and quick iterations, solutions for the needs identified emerge. These solutions are validated step by step by gathering user feedback. As shown in *Figure 3.4* below, in many ways, design thinking allows converting the needs/insights identified into concepts and solutions which constitute the necessary input for product development. Design thinking comprises four main phases:

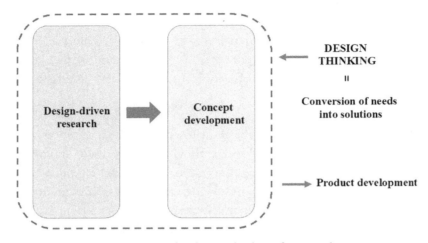

*Figure 3.4: The design thinking framework.*

- A period of observation which provides context and data to an idea generation step where divergence is critical for developing a broad set of hypotheses.
- A phase of understanding the information at hand to create valuable insights.
- These insights will lead to a stage of convergence, where suggestions will be made to address the insights collected.
- The last step will create prototypes representing some of the critical hypotheses that need validation before proceeding to a phase of product development.

*Figure 3.5* below summarizes this process. While design thinking focuses on identifying user needs and validating a solution, it is essential to maintain the right balance between desirability (needs), viability (business potential), and feasibility (is the technology available or can it be developed?). It is important to note that the four phases above do not need to follow a specific order. These phases represent the activities that happen in the innovation process involving design thinking, rather than ordered steps to follow. Design thinking is, by its nature, a non-linear process which is carried out in a flexible way depending on the learnings that occur and the resources available. Some people often refer to it as a mindset, which can be used to focus on any challenge. Design thinking is well suited to situations which are not led by technology or engineering and when the cost (and waste of time) of a failed project development/launch can be substantial.

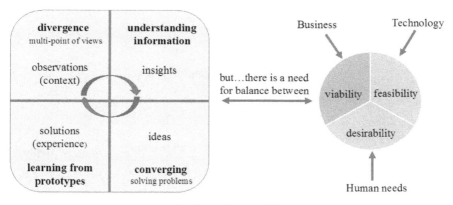

*Figure 3.5: The four phases of design thinking.*

The prototyping phase generally starts by a prototype called "*the dark horse prototype*," which prevents the design space from shrinking too rapidly by bringing optimizations too early. The dark horse prototype aims at trying something "out there," which may seem impossible because it represents a radical departure solution which is risky, but which can be refined enough to be objectively tested.

## 3.7. AGILE DEVELOPMENT

Agile software development is an approach that prioritizes collaboration over documentation, flexibility over strict management practices, and the ability to manage constant change rather than locking yourself into a rigid development process. These days every software development organization seems to practice the agile software development methodology or a version of it. This approach has been replacing the traditional waterfall development methodology, which requires much documentation up front before doing any coding and comprehensive functional specifications, which are, in general, not validated by customer feedback. In contrast, agile development (see *Figure 3.6*) focuses on customer collaboration instead of contract negotiations and responds to changes instead of following a plan. Most of the time, this results in better-quality applications, faster development, and better technical practices.

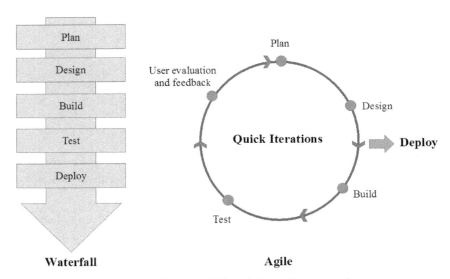

*Figure 3.6: The waterfall and the agile approaches.*

Waterfall development makes sense when the software development is large and complex and requires much discipline, such as large Information Technology (IT) programs at the Department of Defense (DOD). In this case, the outcome of software development is clear, and the pace of change tends to be slow. The central assumption for the software is that it will not change. However, with the Internet era and the time to market always accelerating, for many projects, these assumptions are no longer valid. Developers need a faster and more flexible way to software development, such as agile development which is often synonymous with "build smarter, ship faster."

Agile development delivers results on an iterative schedule where commitments involve small chunks of work (called sprints in the Scrum agile development methodology) which have been decided in advance. These developments can change depending on the results, the feedback obtained from users or the Quality Assurance (QA) team, or changes in requirements. Sprints generally last a few weeks, typically one to four weeks. The work is very collaborative, and delays, challenges, and misjudgments arise early and, if need be, can be addressed in a timely way.

The agile development method begins with a user or customer in mind and somebody in the team (usually called the product owner) which represents the voice of the customer. This person is in charge of providing customer insights and feedback and of creating a product vision. The team is generally a multidisciplinary team composed of a diverse group of people with the skills to get the job done.

There are many agile development frameworks which provide specifics on the methodology and facilitate the software development life cycle. Scrum and Kanban are among the most popular ones. The Scrum methodology focuses on delivering small chunks of work, where daily standup meetings are used to communicate status updates and discuss strategies. The Kanban approach emphasizes user stories which define a staged development process until completion. Among developers, the Scrum methodology appears to be the most widely adopted.

## 3.8.   LEAN INNOVATION

In the last ten years, there have been many books and articles describing the lean startup process and lean innovation (Ries, 2011) (Blank & Dorf, 2012) (Humble, Molesky, & O'Reilly, 2015). Lean innovation focuses on minimizing the risks of failure by capturing customer feedback early and often, and reducing unnecessary developments within the product development cycle. Lean approaches prioritize experimentation, learning, and the gathering of evidence. It relies on continuous validated improvements and testing new concepts and hypotheses very quickly. Lean innovation is a combination of two methodologies:

- The identification of new opportunities, thanks to the gathering of evidence and insights, with processes similar to the ones used in design thinking.
- The agile development method, such as rapid prototyping and quick iteration, to eliminate waste and create validation speed for the hypotheses or opportunities identified.

In many ways, lean innovation and design thinking have strong similarities. Both approaches focus on the customer to identify the problem and gather early customer feedback while developing and validating the concepts developed. As shown in *Figure 3.7*, in contrast with design thinking, lean innovation focuses on the creation of a new business, starts with the vision of the startup founder in mind and is driven by the urgency for the startup not to run out of money, which drives innovation speed. Both design thinking and lean innovation work for large companies. However, for startups, design thinking does not always create the necessary sense of urgency. Design thinking is generally well suited to situations where the process isn't technology driven, and time and money are not a problem.

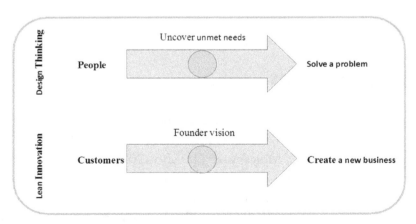

*Figure 3.7: Design thinking versus lean innovation.*

Lean innovation came to the forefront thanks to Steve Blank—co-author of *The Startup Owner's Manual* (Blank & Dorf, 2012) and widely considered as the father of this approach—and Eric Ries, author of the *Lean Startup* (Ries, 2011). Lean innovation enables companies to test hypotheses and build better products faster with fewer resources. At first, rather than money, the critical element is speed and what you can learn from your potential customers. Lean innovation focuses on identifying and building an MVP, which again is the most stripped-down version of a product that early adopters are willing to buy. The MVP has the core features that target customers want, and it serves as a guide for future developments. For testing and validating the business model iteratively, many startups use the business model canvas (Osterwalder & Pigneur, Business Model Generation, 2010) which summarizes, in a very concise way, how a business model creates, delivers, and captures value.

## 3.9. THE POWER OF COLLABORATIVE INNOVATION

In today's quick-to-market and complex world, companies cannot do everything alone. Traditionally, many companies used their internal knowledge to develop products that they often launched globally. However, it is now well accepted that innovation requires different viewpoints, different skill sets, and that collaboration is a way to enhance the internal skill sets. Open innovation has been complementing and sometimes replacing closed approaches to accelerate innovation and create speed and diversity. This changing mindset has enabled many companies to innovate better and faster. People who work in a collaborative environment view seeking help internally or externally as natural regardless of whether or not providing guidance or support is part of the formal job description of the person who is trying to help them.

Partnerships enable companies to act faster, accelerate the time to market, improve the created value, and ultimately create economic growth. Partnerships and collaborations can take different forms.

Apple, for example, built many business relationships by developing an ecosystem, giving birth to the App Store and the development of applications by external developers. One of the keys to partnerships is understanding how building partnerships can help you in meeting customer needs better and faster.

Collaborative innovation creates value. It requires skills and a deep understanding of how to develop successful partnerships by leveraging each other's strengths. Companies often underestimate these skills. Most of the time, successful partnerships involve trust rather than a well-defined and organized process. Japanese companies often build trust via repeated face-to-face meetings before developing cooperative partnerships. The experience shows that one of the keys is to build indispensable relationships. However, in practice, these relationships are challenging to create. Frequently, a lack of trust puts more focus on negotiating than on gaining more value from the relationship.

Collaborative innovation is a hot topic in the B2B space, but it is also prevalent for B2C where growth can be accelerated by co-creating with customers. One of the challenges is how to integrate customers into the innovation process, and for large companies, it's how to fit co-innovation with customers into the operational structure. However, this is easier to say than to execute. Many companies are saying that they are putting their customers at the center of their innovation process, but there is still a big gap between this assertion and their actions. Instead of leveraging customers to guide innovation, many companies unconsciously regard the customer as a distraction.

Collaborative innovation has many advantages. When co-innovating with customers, it allows the organization to build more customer-centric products, to gather meaningful insights but also to minimize risks by getting a better understanding of the market before launching a product. Finally, it helps organizations develop brand loyalty as it creates strong relationships with your potential customers by fostering a sense of ownership.

## 3.10. THE SEARCH AND EXECUTION PHASES: DIFFERENCES BETWEEN STARTUPS AND LARGE CORPORATIONS

Many of the previous sections concentrated on the search phase of the innovation process. While differences exist, the search phase is quite similar between startups and large companies. As described in the previous sections, there is often a greater sense of urgency for startups as their resources and runway are more limited than that of large companies. The innovation process—the generation of ideas, rapid prototyping, the use of design thinking or lean innovation, and validating with customers—fits well with both types of organizations. Startups are bolder, more agile, and excel at searching the innovation space, while corporations are often slowed down by their organization structure.

The big difference between startups and large corporations lies in the transition between the search phase and the execution phase. Large corporations often have a hard time between the search phase and the execution phase, as the current business is getting in the way of the new one. While innovation and R&D teams are usually doing a good job at generating new ideas, concepts, and opportunities, many of these new opportunities fall in the "Death Valley of Innovation." The main reason is that traditional activities, processes, directions, and previous successes are taking precedence over more bold and novel directions. In these large companies, middle management is generally responsible for stopping innovation. Due to their inability to take risks and the lack of aligned incentives, middle managers end up taking a safe approach protecting the current business at the expense of innovation.

On the other hand, large corporations are very well suited to execute. They have processes in place, the support staff (e.g., legal and logistics) trained and ready for enabling successful business operations from lessons learned via previous successful experiences. Startups have to set up these processes and need to scale on the fly, hiring resources as required, raising funds and making mistakes along the way. It is one of the significant challenges that startups face. For startups, one way to mitigate this risk is to surround themselves (e.g., via an advisory board) with people who have the experience of having done this in the past so that they can minimize possible mistakes as they navigate unknown territories.

Regarding the search phase, it is essential to realize that there is no innovation without experimentation and that experimentation comes at a cost. Startups have a strong incentive to do an excellent job during the experimentation phase because otherwise, they may run out of funds. Large corporations usually do not have this problem, but they are often afraid to fail as they are addicted to predictability. Though they have the runway to think long term, they often focus on the loss that may occur in the short term and consequently may not try to experiment. They usually manage innovation the same way they operate their core business and by doing so are making the wrong decisions. Large corporations should focus on a long-term approach that will allow them to use their resources and time to experiment. Innovation necessitates a different mindset, a different way to mitigate risk, and it is entirely different from execution and traditional ROI mindset. The ROI of experimentation is insight and learning. It has value, and large corporations must improve on this. Instead of focusing on a rigorous process well adapted to predictability, they need to embrace innovation, which is inherently an unpredictable process.

# CHAPTER 4

## Funding a Startup— Developing and Executing a Successful Funding Strategy

### 4.1. OUTLINE OF THE VENTURE CAPITAL INVESTING PROCESS

To be able to create a new business you need three essential components:

- Talented people to make it happen.
- Innovative products/services.
- A market which accepts the products/services.

Among the above, while people are replaceable and product/services can be improved, a suitable market must be present. Venture Capitalists (VCs) and angel investors are looking for the three components above, emphasizing the three elements differently. However, they always look for significant market potential.

Typically, VCs provide strategic assistance, access to their network, and introductions to potential customers and partners. They are usually investing in specific segments or industries, are specialized in one or more startup stages such as Pre-Seed, Seed, or Series A, and sometimes favor certain geographies (e.g., Silicon Valley or the United

States). Today there is more capital available than there used to be, and startups tend to stay private longer. The fact that more capital is available is pushing VCs to try to differentiate themselves to provide more value. The funding rounds tend to be larger because VCs are aiming for faster growth. Companies such as Uber and Lyft exemplify it. For example, when Lyft filed for IPO, they were generating more than two billion dollars in revenue, and had a loss of more than 900 million dollars (O'Donnell & Franklin, 2019) while raising seven billion dollars for new funds from Genstar Capital. Investors have been willing to pour in billions of dollars because they believe those losses will eventually evaporate. It is all about growth and scale.

Raising venture capital is not easy and requires many meetings and pitches with potential investors before finding one who can help you and is interested in investing in your company. Before approaching a potential investor, it is essential for a startup to do its homework and to be well prepared. It requires a strong investor pitch deck emphasizing the problem you are solving, the solution developed, the unique value proposition, the traction obtained, the significant market size and the go-to-market strategy. Investors are hard to get to as they get many solicitations from interested startups. So, the best way to get in touch with investors is through a warm introduction from a trusted acquaintance who knows both the startup and the investor. Often another fellow entrepreneur, who was invested in by the firm you are seeking capital from, can be a good choice. He/she can also fill you in about the kind of investment and support the investor can provide.

If the meetings with the potential investor and his/her partners from the VC firm are successful, then discussions about valuation, term sheet, and due diligence take place, before drafting legal documents which will outline the investment. The whole process can be very time consuming and generally takes at least several months to complete.

The term sheet is an important document which covers all of the essential conditions of the financing such as the startup valuation, control issues such as participation on the Board of Directors, rights to participate in future financing rounds and what kind approval or "veto" rights the investors will have. The term sheet could be brief (short form) or more detailed (extended version) depending on whether it covers only the most critical points or all the details that will need an agreement. While short forms are usually used to agree on the essential items, all the details will need to be covered in an extended term sheet before the investment takes place. Typically, the investment uses one of the following vehicles:

- Convertible promissory note, issued by the company to the investor, convertible into the company stock in the next round of financing.
- Simple Agreement for Future Equity (SAFE), first developed by Y Combinator, which is an alternative to convertible notes often used in Silicon Valley. Unlike a note, a SAFE has no maturity date and does not bear interest. Founders should be aware of the modifications made to SAFE in 2018, where the new SAFE deals with post-money valuation (Adeeb, 2018).
- Convertible preferred stocks which give investors a preference over common stocks on the sale of the company and have the upside potential of being able to convert to common stocks of the company.

The composition of the board of directors is usually a critical discussion point between investors and startup founders. The board of directors monitors the progress of the company, approves directions and crucial decisions, and plays a meaningful role in the running of the business. It could be a contentious negotiation point as founders want to keep the control of the company and investors want to be able to monitor their investment and make sure that they can play an active role going forward in the critical decisions. Usually, the allocation of board seats follows the share ownership.

Many more investment provisions need to be negotiated between founders and investors, such as protective provisions and veto rights of the investors, anti-dilution protection, stock options, and pool issues. The goal of this section is not to provide an exhaustive list and detailed information that the startup founder needs to pay attention to and understand, but rather it is to outline some of the critical steps of the venture capital investment process. More information is available in the book from Alejandro Cremades: *The Art of Startup Fundraising: Pitching Investors, Negotiating the Deal, and Everything Else Entrepreneurs Need to Know* (Cremades, 2016).

## 4.2. THE DIFFERENT FUNDING SOURCES

Startup founders looking to raise funds can look into different funding sources. The appropriate funding source depends on the stage of the startup, how much money it wants to raise, and what type of help it needs from an investor, besides the funds it wants to raise. Funding sources include the following categories:

- Bootstrap fund/self-funding.
- Friends and family.
- Government grants and other similar programs (e.g., EU framework programs for startups in Europe).
- Loans (e.g., from banks).
- Angel investors and high net worth individuals.
- Incubators and accelerators.
- VCs.
- Strategic investors (e.g., corporations).

This list does not include crowdsourcing, which will be described separately in the following section because crowdsourcing combines its ability to raise funds with a way to test and validate a market and a demand.

Usually bootstrapping with the founders' money or family and friends' funding provides only enough to create a proof of concept and mainly applies to small-scale enterprises/projects. As at this point, the company valuation is low, and it is best to limit the funding to what is needed to get to the next stage. Funding of roughly $100K is typical at this stage. Bootstrapping allows the entrepreneur to focus on obtaining the validation and traction necessary to be attractive for equity investment later.

Government programs and bank loans are other sources of funds that founders should consider. One of the advantages is that founders do not trade the funds for equity. However, bank loans need to be repaid, with accrued interest, and generally introduce a high risk of collateral loss, as it is a requirement for loans. Government programs as an initial source of funding have been popular in European countries (due to EU framework programs and local/national support to startups) and Asian countries such as Japan (with research programs such as NEDO).

Angel investors are organized groups of high net worth individuals (prevalent in Silicon Valley, e.g., Sand Hill Angels). High net worth individuals invest periodically in areas of interest. Once committed, the turn around to close the deal can be quick and negotiations simple, as often the specific area the startup is working on and the problem that they are solving takes precedence over the startup valuation. Angel investors are willing to take risks on business ideas and hope for a good return on their investment. The amount of funding provided typically ranges from $100K to $750K. For some of the business angel groups, the amount of funding can go to $1.5M. However, the higher the funding level, the more due diligence is required, and the more negotiation there is around valuation and other conditions from the term sheet.

Joining an incubator or accelerator can also be a way to raise some funding (typically around $100K) and get accelerated via mentorship, coaching, introduction to possible partners and funding sources, in exchange for roughly 5% to 7% of equity. Some accelerators such as Plug and Play, a Silicon Valley-based startup accelerator, do not require a portion of the company because their corporate partners sponsor the accelerator program. However, the selection process to get accepted in the accelerator can be quite competitive. It also requires a firm commitment from the startup for the acceleration period (several months), as such a program is generally very intense.

For VCs who raise their capital to invest from limited partners, the rate of ROI is critical. They tend to come later in the funding rounds and typically participate with investments of several million dollars. Due diligence takes time (it is not unusual to take several months and up to six months), and discussions around valuation are thorough. VCs effectively monitor the progress of the company they invest in, thus ensuring the sustainability and growth of their investment. When dealing with VCs, it is crucial to raise only the needed funds and not more, as the funds raised can be expensive in terms of the equity provided in exchange. It is generally a good idea to look for "smart money," meaning you need to understand what the venture capital firm you are selecting can do for you beyond the funds they are providing in terms of, for example, introductions and strategic guidance. The startup founder should be careful not to lose control of the business since the founder is giving up equity to investors.

The last category of investors is strategic investors. It includes the venture groups of large corporations who are investing in startups, usually taking minority stakes, not with ROI as the prime motivator, but rather with prioritizing strategic issues such as internal collaborations with their business divisions. In this case, the corporation can also provide strategic benefits to the startup and access to corporate resources such as their customers, channels, and brand. However, the startup needs to understand that this can, in some cases, reduce the potential for an exit (e.g., from an Initial Public Offering [IPO] or a trade sale) with another party other than the strategic investor. Also, the startup should be careful about the rights granted to the strategic investor (e.g., right of first refusal) as it can make the next funding rounds difficult if the startup is not careful.

*Figure 4.1* summarizes these funding sources together with the typical milestones and funding size associated with each round of funding, though outliers exist. There is much more to the funding sources than what we described above. The previous sections provide a simple summary of what a startup needs to consider when looking for funding. Before raising money, it is generally a good idea to talk to several fellow entrepreneurs who went through different rounds to understand the dos and don'ts, along with obtaining first-hand information about the investors considered. Bootstrapping, among other funding sources, is the best way to kick off your new venture. However, additional funding sources are worth considering at the appropriate stage of the startup to attain the next step, accelerate traction, and create speed to win the market.

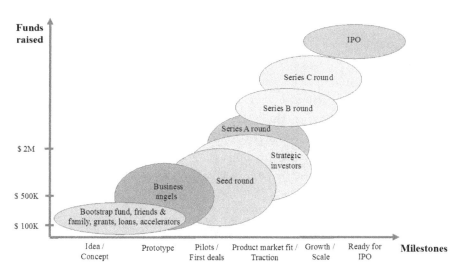

*Figure 4.1: Funding sources, typical milestones, and funding sizes.*

## 4.3. CROWDFUNDING YOUR STARTUP

Crowdfunding (Stegmaier, 2015) is a new funding mechanism created in April 2012 where companies can raise funds in 12 months that can reach $1M without the requirement to sell securities to only accredited investors. Crowdfunding platforms are set up for individuals to pitch their ideas or business to people who are willing to support them. Using a crowdfunding platform (such as Kickstarter or Indiegogo) the company shares the description of what they offer, their business model, and their potential for growth. If the crowdfunders on the platform like what they see, they can pledge to support the company by donating funds often in exchange for equity or reward (the two most popular models shown in *Figure 4.2*), such as a future product that the company will release or some other in-kind benefits.

For the startup, besides the funds raised, crowdfunding provides a way to evaluate the public interest for its business (similar to free marketing). It also allows the startup to capture early adopters and finance its product development, without having to give up equity (for the reward model). Furthermore, a successful crowdfunding campaign may make it easier, later on, to attract further investment. Crowdfunding makes use of a network of people through social media and other communities to bring individual investors and entrepreneurs together. However, it also creates some risks such as: the threat of having the ideas stolen (if no protection, such as patents, exists); exposure of early ideas to competitors, who may be able to implement the product or a variant faster; or—for the supporters—the possibility of fraud, e.g. if the promised rewards do not materialize.

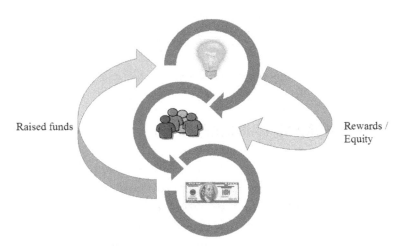

*Figure 4.2: The crowdfunding mechanism.*

The reward system is one of the most popular models with platforms such as Kickstarter (www.kickstarter.com) and Indiegogo (www.indiegogo.com). Supporters can choose the monetary extent of their support, and they receive rewards in return. The more money they spend, the more they gain. Credibility for the reward crowdfunding model comes from delivering a product that works, on time. However, experience often shows, the delivery of the products is late as many entrepreneurs underestimate the complexity of product development and delivery. The reward model works well for consumer products as supporters provide a certain amount of funding in exchange for receiving the product as if they were pre-ordering it.

The equity model (like the platform Fundable.com) is less popular than the reward model, mainly because startups want to limit who invests and to whom they can transfer shares. It can also make a company challenging to fund for the next rounds as a company that raised money from hundreds of investors is likely to scare off institutional investors.

When starting a campaign, it is essential to encourage interest in it using any means you have at your disposal. Ideally, you have created an audience in advance with E-mails, blogs, and social networks. It means that you have to create a marketing plan before launching your campaign. The more friends, followers, and readers you have, the more chances you have of raising money for your project. You need to contact them in advance and persuade them to participate in your project. Typically, with crowdfunding 20 to 30% of the amount raised comes from friends and acquaintances mobilized before starting the campaign.

## 4.4. TALKING TO AN INVESTOR—THE DOS AND DON'TS

Having meetings with investors is not always easy and often leads to high-pressure situations. However, experience shows that being authentic and honest is the best way to approach such meetings. Below is a compilation of things to do and not to do during these meetings.

Starting from the things that investors always appreciate, below is a list of helpful tips.

- Be prepared. It is essential to be ready to share your financials, your knowledge of the market, information about your team, the way you are approaching the opportunity and the position of your company as compared to the competition. You should also have a clear action plan about how to address your problems and challenges.
- Be honest, be yourself, and do not embellish. It is essential to be upfront about where you are, your challenges, and how you see the future instead of giving the impression that everything is under control or that there is no competition. Assessing in complete honesty where you are along with your challenges is a sign of humility and maturity.
- Be clear and prepared about how you will use the investment. Investors want to give money to a team that can make the most of it and has a clear purpose for it. Be prepared to justify the amount that you are putting forward. It is also essential to talk in phases, meaning outlining milestones that you want to reach and what will happen after you achieve them. Investors are familiar with a phase-based investment strategy and are likely to appreciate this approach.
- Develop a roadmap outlining clearly how each milestone will improve the value proposition and help to capture a more substantial part of the market.
- Do not be afraid to say no to some of their suggestions. Investors are also trying to evaluate you as a leader, along with your ability to execute and to grow.
- Do not be afraid to ask questions. Showing your curiosity, willingness to learn, and leadership is a good thing.
- Be precise, unambiguous, and concise. Do not ramble.
- Get to know your investors and determine if they are a good fit for you. It is a two-way street, and assessing if your

investors can be good partners you can trust and who can help you grow is very important.

- Let investors learn about you. Investors want to know you and your team, see your passion and understand if you can execute.

When talking to an investor, there are also several mistakes that a founder wants to avoid. Some of the common ones are listed below:

- Do not speak all the time. Be mindful about what investors want to know and listen carefully to what they have to say. You do not have to follow every piece of advice that investors give you, but being a good listener is often a quality that investors appreciate.
- Do not ask for an NDA. Investors never sign NDAs, as they get in contact with many similar companies all the time.
- Do not talk about exits. More than monetary gains, investors want to see your passion and drive, and a strong motivation for the problem that you are trying to solve.
- Do not talk to the wrong investor. Do your homework and research the area the investors you want to talk to invest in, what are the startup stages (e.g., Seed, Series A) the investors focus on, and what other entrepreneurs can tell you about them.
- Do not think that investors are smarter than you about your business just because of their experience meeting many startups. Everybody has his/her own bias. In the end, while you want to listen, it is also essential to follow your passion and not to give up, if you believe that this is the way to go.
- Do not share all the details about your company upfront. Give your investors a chance to dig deeper if they want to.
- Do not bring many of your team members to an investor meeting. Most of the time, one of the founders, especially for the first meeting, is enough.
- Do not project your growth based on similar past success. Every situation is different, and execution is often the determining factor for success or failure.

In the end, you want to build trusted relationships with your investors. It is not about just pitching at your investors. It is about finding out on both sides if there is a good fit. Make sure that you are not seeing your investors as only a source of funds but rather value them as a source of input on your company, if you are going to partner with them. If they are not a good fit, it is a good practice to express your gratitude for them listening to you and for their time. It is a small world, and along the way, you never know what kind of help you will need.

## 4.5. YOUR FUNDING STRATEGY

Raising capital can be hard for founders. Two of the main reasons are lack of a suitable network and lack of financial literacy. One of the most common mistakes for startup founders is not to develop an appropriate funding strategy. The consequences of poor planning can be substantial dilution, a founder with little control over the business, or a smaller upside on exit. Based on the experience of many entrepreneurs, some of the errors often made are:

- Taking too much money too soon. The earlier you take the money, the more expensive it is. Besides this, raising more money to reach a given milestone may sometimes lead to poor decisions.
- Running out of money due to not raising enough funds.
- Forming a wrong opinion about the investor and taking money from the wrong investor, which could lead to conflicts or very little help beyond the funds received.
- Misjudging between convertible debt, preferred stocks, or common stocks in exchange for the funding received. Funding for startups is available in many different forms, and a founder should consider what is best for each stage of the business. As the company evolves and grows, some types of capital are more appropriate than others. Mentors or other

entrepreneurs with experience in fundraising could be a good place to start when seeking advice.

Creating a sound funding strategy means establishing a set of milestones for the growth of the company and developing a funding strategy that is in line with the roadmap accomplishments. Funds need to be raised to go from one milestone to the next. By taking the right amount of money at the right time from the appropriate investors, a startup will maximize its chance of success. It often means aligning the funding raised with the burn rate for the headcount to reach the next product milestones, business development, including sales and marketing, along with legal and other fees such as office expansion.

The milestones defined should be measurable and generally paired with increased traction. *Figure 4.3* below shows two of the most important landmarks, namely achieving the product–market fit and demonstrating a repeatable and scalable sales model/customer acquisition. As the traction increases, so do the valuation and the amount of money that will be part of the next round of funding. When raising a new funding round, it is essential to be patient. The key is to understand the different options available and to figure out who the investors are that will fit best with your startup and the stage of your company. Funding your startup is always a critical component to your business venture and a significant challenge to tackle. However, raising money does not equal business success. It is only one essential component of a successful venture. Though it is a critical component, it can be less challenging to raise money than to get paying customers. Real success comes from selling your product to many customers!

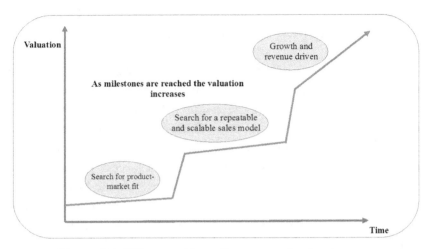

*Figure 4.3: When reaching milestones, valuation increases.*

## 4.6. CASH IS KING

At the macro level, one of the most critical roles of a startup CEO is to make sure that the startup does not run out of cash; otherwise, the startup will not be able to survive. Managing the cash flow means being very aware of strict deadlines that you need to meet and the milestones that you need to achieve to be able to reach the next stage and raise the next rounds of funding at ever-increasing valuations. Time is of the essence, along with a clear focus to make sure that the amount of cash at hand is optimized to reach the milestones. If you want to maximize your chances of success, it is essential to adopt one of the two following strategies:

- Raise enough funding to meet your roadmap development.
- Match your milestones to the available cash.

Depending on the current state of the startup, the founder will choose one strategy or another. If the startup is already in a fundraising phase, the first strategy is the most appropriate, while if the startup has already raised funds, the second strategy makes sense, though raising more cash in some instances could be an alternative.

In some cases, the startup has already raised funds, but it realizes that a milestone may be hard to achieve with the amount of cash at hand. In this case, the startup could either reduce the burn rate to allow the completion of the milestone before running out of money or, in agreement with the startup investors, could determine a different set of achievements that will still enable raising an up round—a round of financing in which the startup's worth increased since its previous valuation—successfully. It is essential for the founders to understand how the startups are valued (see the next section). One of the things that the founders want to avoid is to have a down round as this signals that the startup is not performing according to expectations. A down round can have significant adverse effects on hiring, sales, or the next round of funding.

It is always a good idea to validate with investors that the milestones you planned for are sufficient to raise your next round of funding at an increased valuation. Executing these milestones should be the primary focus of the company, considering the cash at hand as this sets a real constraint for the startup. It is vital for the startup not to be distracted from reaching the milestones as the cost of failure is either a down round or closing the company.

## 4.7. UNDERSTANDING STARTUP VALUATION

The startup valuation is a critical issue to agree upon between the entrepreneur and the investor. They need to reach an agreement on the "pre-money valuation," which is the value of the company before the investment. For example, as shown in *Figure 4.4*, if the investor plans to invest $5M in a financing round where the pre-money valuation is $20M, that means that the "post-money" valuation is $25M and that the investor aims at obtaining 20% of the company (5/25) at the closing of the financing.

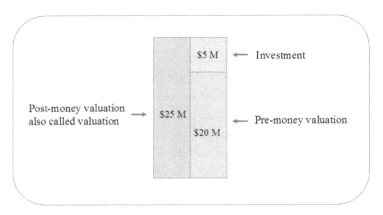

*Figure 4.4: The pre and post-money valuation.*

Startup valuations are directly related to an estimation of risk and reward. They increase as the level of risk goes down (or as the size of the anticipated return goes up). Many factors influence how to determine the pre-money valuation (Poland, 2014), and it is negotiable. This determination is subjective, and it is more an art than a science. Some of these factors include:

- Current traction and revenues.
- The size of the market opportunity.
- The unique value proposition, and if the technology is proprietary and protected.
- The valuation of comparable companies (e.g., similar stage, similar industry).
- The popularity of the area, and the current economic conditions.

The higher the valuation, the less the dilution for the founders. From an investor perspective, a lower estimation will result in a higher percentage of the company and potentially a more significant upside down the road.

Multiple of revenues is one of the methods to assist in determining the valuation of a company. However, this approach is most appropriate for later stage companies. For early-stage companies, including companies raising a Series A round, the current stage of the company and how it compares to that of similar companies constitutes an alternative. As a justification, it is always a good idea for the founders to research companies in their space, understand their traction (though it can be challenging to obtain this information) and to create a comparative table positioning their startup with these companies. While subjective, this method is often used to get a preliminary estimation of the valuation. Determining it is unique for each company and it is based on both tangible (e.g., how long the company took to bootstrap) and intangible (experience of the founders) criteria.

Typically, early-stage companies get valuations based on their stage. For example, the range of pre-money valuation for friends and family rounds is generally no more than $1M, for angel rounds, it is usually in the $1M-$5M range, and for institutional rounds, it is typically in the $5M-$15M range. These are just some guidelines, which of course vary according to each particular situation.

Regarding the pre-money value, the founders need to view the investment from the investor's perspective. Investors are looking for investments that minimize their risk, and that have a potential for tremendous upside. So, the founders need to create strategies to de-risk the investment, for example:

- Limiting the execution risk by having already assembled a strong team.
- Having demonstrated traction and a product-market fit. If you can walk into an investor meeting with a list of 20 customers that are willing to talk to investors, your chances of getting funded will go up substantially, and your valuation will likely increase.
- Having filed for intellectual property protection or demonstrating a path toward market sustainability via clear barriers to entry.
- Addressing a large market with a business model that provides good margins.

It is sometimes not easy for a startup to satisfy all these points. Investors will look for intermediate milestones to help reduce the risk. For the entrepreneur, it is not always good to end up with a high valuation, as, if too high, it may make the next round of financing difficult. As already discussed, it is essential to avoid a down round, which could happen if you are not able to justify, down the line, the post-money valuation. Strategic and careful planning, executing according to milestones and setting up realistic estimates, are the things that the entrepreneur needs to pay attention to, to make sure that the next financing rounds will be up rounds.

## 4.8. BEYOND THE FUNDS: WHAT TO LOOK FOR IN A FUNDING PARTNER

Before selecting the right funding partner, it is critical to know as much as possible about the person/entity who is investing in your startup. You should do your due diligence and take time to learn about your investor. Some of the questions that the founder should answer are:

- Are you compatible with the investor? What is your chemistry with the investor leading the deal?
- What is the reputation of the investor (this can influence future financing rounds)?
- What are the other companies the investor already invested in, and how are they doing?
- Did the investor make non-monetary contributions to these companies?
- Did the investor stick with these companies when they were in trouble?
- Does the investor understand your industry?
- Does the investor have the network and reputation for attracting other potential investors (e.g., for the next financing round) or partners?

While this list is not exhaustive, the primary objective is to look for compatibility, value, and shared goals with the investor. Of course, all the above is in addition to the economics of the deal, which is often what the entrepreneur has first in mind when looking for an investment.

## 4.9. FUNDING A STARTUP WHICH IS A CORPORATION SPIN-OFF

A spin-off is a new company formed from an existing one. It is an uncommon startup. Spin-offs are often attractive to investors for the following reasons:

- They are usually aiming at substantial market opportunities.
- Benefitting from the large corporation that created them, these spin-offs focus on viable products, and investors can more readily trust the startup. Spin-offs also often leverage technology that has been tried and tested.
- They usually come with a strong management team and may be able to leverage many corporate resources.

The more attractive a startup appears to investors, the more the company can negotiate its terms. There are not only financial benefits when spinning off a company. Other advantages include rallying the company employees around a single mission, which can also be important for customers, and associating a definite value to one name. So, clarity, focus, purpose, and avoiding the distractions that come from the large corporation are also elements to consider.

However, large corporations often choose to incubate and *spin-in* startups as a new entity, or a new division or business unit. The process usually necessitates the support financially and politically at a high executive level in the company. While the corporation may have good intentions and the financial resources to do this, the organizational structure of large corporations, the different incentives offered, personal interests, and political motivations are often going against the internal venture at some point or another, resulting in the death of the spin-in entity. The mechanisms of decisions, Key Performance Indicators (KPIs), and the past success of large companies are often going against creating something new with a completely different approach. Large companies need to unlearn, and it is challenging to do it while conducting today's business.

# CHAPTER 5

## Building Effective Relationships and Collaborations

## 5.1.  BUILDING A STARTUP: THE IMPORTANCE OF RELATIONSHIPS

While many entrepreneurs work very hard to succeed, it is generally the case that their relationships and how these evolve are more central to their success than their hard work and long hours. Developing the right connections and avoiding those who can harm your business are critical skills to develop. Even when a startup has the best technology or business model, it will often be difficult to succeed without having developed successful relationships. It necessitates clear communication and a will to seek win–win partnerships. Effectively building relationships is a skill that you can learn, even if you are an introvert. It does take focus and effort, and it is a skill that you can develop over time.

Relationships that can be trusted are not easy to build and often take time, but this often becomes a critical competitive advantage, sometimes undervalued. Today, even more than before, we are living in a collaborative world, a customer-driven environment where networking is king. It requires a strong effort from everyone involved to develop sustainable, productive, and effective relationships.

With the multitude of things that an entrepreneur has to do and to worry about, quality relationships are often the last concerns of the startup founder. However, understanding that not all connections are equal, managing them and prioritizing the important ones is an essential skill for an entrepreneur.

The path of an entrepreneur is full of uncertainties. Building a new business requires all the support that you can get. It helps you, as you can leverage the experience that you do not have and build confidence to hit your milestones. When things are getting challenging, you may need the extra boost from positive relationships that will recognize your talent and ability at a time where you may be doubting yourself. This extra boost can make a surprisingly significant difference in the outcome.

Business relationships can be complicated and often need a strong foundation. Respect, mutual admiration, and the recognition that over time and together, you will be able to overcome the challenges are all critical ingredients to overcome difficulties. Building positive and trusted relationships, personally or for your business, should never take a backseat. Make them part of your entrepreneurial journey.

## 5.2. DEVELOPING THE NETWORK FOR YOUR STARTUP TO SUCCEED

The right connections will help you form partnerships and can change the entire course of your company. However, starting to build these connections when you are also establishing your business is too late and can be very challenging. The earlier you can start the better. Whatever you do in life, you always need to build, strengthen, and improve your network. Powerful connections will make a difference in your life.

Your network should be composed of a variety of people with diverse backgrounds and experience. When building a business, as illustrated in *Figure 5.1*, it is essential to have contacts and build relationships with the following people:

- Potential targeted customers. They will enable you to get early feedback, validate the problem that you want to solve and benefit from a pool of early adopters who will guide your next steps. Without these initial connections, starting a business can take time. If you do not have these connections, partnering with a person or company, who can help you with introductions, makes much sense.

- Investors. As mentioned earlier, investors put much weight on the team and their ability to execute. If you have built trusted and positive relationships with investors, it can help you tremendously to raise the funds that you need to grow your startup.

- Partners/Collaborators. As your startup grows, and even at the beginning, you may not have the resources, the experience, or the expertise to tackle all the challenges that come your way. Being able to find the right partner, the right talents, and the appropriate innovation ecosystem to accelerate how you go to market or scale can be invaluable. It can help speed up your growth as gaining experience for things you have never done or do not have the resources to do can be too much for you. It is often the case when timing and speed are critical.

- Media/PR. Having the right contacts with media or PR companies can help increase visibility for your company and help you gain traction. If you do not have these contacts, partnering with a marketing firm who has these contacts in the industry you are working within can help you quickly reach journalists and advocates who could spread the word.

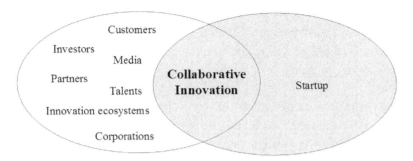

*Figure 5.1: Developing your network for collaborative innovation.*

It is essential to understand that these relationships take time to develop and cannot happen instantaneously. It is a lifelong commitment and an investment that should be part of your journey and shape what you are doing now and in the future.

You need to put some effort into developing connections and your network. Likewise, providing value to your relationships is critical. As you engage and your community grows, it may be difficult to nurture all your contacts. Connecting via events or community-based gathering can be a way to stay in touch while managing your priorities. In all cases, authenticity, clear communication, and empathy are paramount. Understanding not only your needs but the concerns of the people you meet will create fruitful exchanges that will bring value to both parties and lead to sustained relationships.

It is helpful to renew and reshape your network continuously. While building and developing an extensive set of connections is valuable, more relationships are not always better. Identifying the people that are crucial for the future of your business and establishing a strategy to build these connections is essential. Joining online communities, participating in social events related to your industry, and being active on social media will help you enhance your visibility and connect to people relevant to you and what you want to do. Always remember that it is not about you, but it is about connecting, being curious, and learning about the other person too. Listening and learning—not just selling your solution—goes a long way toward establishing positive relationships.

## 5.3.  BUILDING THE RIGHT MEDIA RELATIONSHIPS

Every startup wants PR and visibility, but getting good PR comes with experience and with developing the right strategies and connections to get there. Most of the time, startups do not have the resources to create a PR/media strategy and initially rely on temporary help when needed. While startups are usually active in using social media, they are not always able to handle more structured gatherings such as industry trade shows and national or global publications. Successful startups can develop relationships with reporters and journalists that increase their chances of getting coverage.

Especially when resources are scarce, social media is often critical to reaching your target audiences. Having some simple tools in place to track what works and does not work is essential to be able to change course quickly when things do not go the way you assumed they would.

Like any relationship, building media connections should not start when a need arises. It should start much earlier as you always need to promote your brand and have news coverage. A startup needs to build a program which is made up of media relations, social media, and content creation, which will help sustain continuous updates and visibility. As mentioned, bringing a PR expert inside the team or with a contractual engagement can be worthwhile. However, picking the right partner is critical as every partner will bring a different level of knowledge for your industry and another personal network.

Media relationships rely on communication. To facilitate the building of a media network and to manage expectations, it is essential to create a PR roadmap. It is also critical for the entrepreneur or the team member talking to the media to be truthful. If you damage the journalist's credibility, you will not get a second chance. Transparency, authenticity, and trust are essential, like in any relationship. For your startup, the benefits of media coverage are multiple. These benefits include:

- Enhancing your brand visibility and reputation and positioning you as a market leader.
- Hiring and talent acquisition.
- Customer acquisition, as content and social media posts will lead people to your website.
- Attracting investors and collaboration partners.

All the above are necessary things that any startup wants to do, and media coverage is an excellent way to trigger and accelerate them. Understanding the value of communication between your startup and the media is essential to achieve your goals, as it will increase your chances of success. In contrast, poor media relations, just like poor customer reviews, can be very detrimental to your business.

## 5.4. VALUING CLOSE RELATIONSHIPS WITH YOUR INVESTORS

Section 4.4 already highlighted the importance of building relationships with investors. Building strong ties with your investors is essential as investors will endorse the growth of the company, provide advice, help with decisions, and make their networks available. This Section further emphasizes the desired entrepreneur characteristics and that as an entrepreneur, it is your responsibility to build and strengthen your ties with investors to position your current and future business ventures for success. Most investors value the following qualities in an entrepreneur:

- Commitment and trust. It is especially important for first-time founders who do not have the business experience yet and rely entirely on external advice. Trust should be earned and deserved. Demonstrating that you are committed to your venture and showing that you give full attention to make the most out of your investors' time goes a long way toward building trust.

- Transparency, authenticity, and integrity. This is the result of honest, respectable communications, and it helps to survive during hard times, which is inevitably the case. Keeping your words, taking the business seriously and being open, while aligning your words and actions are essential ingredients in creating the needed environment.

- Connecting deeply via effective communication. It means listening attentively and not being afraid to disagree when you have a good reason for doing so. It is also good practice to communicate about wins and challenges, to set up clear expectations, especially at the beginning, and to share your passion and vision while listening to their concerns.

For an investor, investing in your startup must not be an "invest and forget" scenario. Investors will often worry if they do not hear from you, frequently and regularly. The founders–investors relationships get tested when your startup stops running smoothly and when difficult decisions are needed. If you feel at any time that your goals and incentives are not aligned, it is important to address the issues and voice your concerns, because the disagreement is often due to miscommunications and inexperience. Strong relationships come from celebrating the wins and going through the hard times together, as when bad times happen, it is an opportunity to get to know your investors more deeply. Getting to know each other as people throughout many difficult challenges gives you the ability to fix things together when you need to.

## 5.5.  BUILDING GOOD RELATIONSHIPS WITH YOUR CUSTOMERS

The foundation of building a successful business is to find customers for whom you can create value and who are willing to pay for the value you bring to them. However, as with investors, you should not only view a customer as a person who is buying your products or services. Building strong relationships with your customers will allow you to create a repeatable business, future referrals, generate ideas for future products and set you up for growth by morphing the demand for your products and services from push (supply) to pull (demand). To create this pull, you need to give full attention to the following aspects of your business:

- Exceptional customer service. Amazon showed very well that exceptional customer service and decreasing or eliminating the friction points between your business and your customers is a winning solution to grow your business.

- Exceptional communication while shortening the time to respond to customer requests. Making your customers comfortable, providing clear signals that you are listening to them and taking care of them, and that their requests are taken seriously goes a long way toward smoothing out some issues, especially initially when you are going to market. Experience shows that, when a problem occurs, more important than the problem itself is the way you handle the problem and take care of the customer.

- Not overpromising and exceeding expectations. One of the best ways to build strong relationships with your customers is not to overpromise and to consistently over-deliver. Setting up realistic expectations about the value that your products or services can bring and delivering according to the expectations you set is critical. Overpromising is counterproductive, and while it may allow you to close a short-term sale, it will not ensure repeatability. In contrast, trying to find an opportunity to surprise your customer by over-delivering or providing a token of appreciation for being your customer is something that builds customer loyalty.

- Be open and be a resource for your customer. To build repeatability and scale into your business, you will need to be credible, and your customers will need to trust you. To this end, remaining open while expressing your opinion—which may be different from that of your customer—with respect and confidence is essential. Sharing your knowledge and expertise while listening to customer concerns is a good practice that will contribute over time to build your reputation and increase your chances that customers will come back to you when needed.

- Ask for feedback and be positive. Whatever their experience is—good or bad—most of the time, customers do not hesitate to let you know what they think. Invite them to share their feedback and make their feeling known as their comments constitute meaningful learning and input for your business. From the customer point of view, understanding that you are seriously listening and that you are taking their feedback makes them more tolerant of the imperfections of your products and increases their satisfaction. Always stay positive, even in the presence of negative feedback, as a positive attitude and enthusiasm is a way to build customer confidence. Negative feedback is precious, sometimes even more than positive feedback as it allows you to change course quickly before it is too late. To elicit honest and valuable feedback, be authentic, and put the highest priority on creating value for your customers.

- Do not always sell or speak about your business; continuously understanding customer needs is important. One of the mistakes that some startups make is that when they go into a selling phase, they stop listening to customers. It is a huge mistake. Startups need to be always ready to change course based on the understanding of their customers. Always finding out what your customers' problems are and showing them that you are working on a solution will go a long way toward satisfying them.

It is often said that the customer is king. Without satisfied and paying customers, there is no business, so paying attention to the above points is vital for building a successful business.

## 5.6.  DRIVING GROWTH VIA COLLABORATIVE INNOVATION

In today's accelerating time to market and in light of the increasing complexity of the problems to solve, it is hard—even for a large corporation—to do everything alone. Collaborative innovation between companies is a process where two or more companies contribute toward developing new products, services, or other collaborative outcomes. This is one powerful way to develop and commercialize new technologies and products or services efficiently, to be able to solve complex problems and to create economic growth. Collaborative innovation drives growth through new (or enhanced) products or services that fulfill or create market demand by creating additional value for companies and their customers. For example, Apple, as a company, has been very good at leveraging partnerships and collaborative innovation for building products like the iPhone or the iPad.

While there is no doubt that collaborative innovation can be beneficial to any company, and it is an excellent way to create value, many find it challenging to execute. Collaboration necessitates non-adversarial mindsets, the ability to adapt, and often new metrics. The following aspects need to be considered to increase your chances of success:

- Aligning early the business expectations, objectives, and motivations of each of the partners.
- Creating a flexible partnership structure which allows the companies to adapt and change course if needed during the partnership, as the execution of the collaboration always requires additional information and discoveries. The more the vision for the alliance is unclear, the more flexible the partnership should be as the partnership conditions and boundaries need to be defined.
- Executing intellectual property agreements which are fair and mutually beneficial. It is sometimes a tough topic to negotiate, especially between a large corporation and a small startup, as large corporations sometimes take advantage of

their scale and resources to negotiate conditions which are difficult to accept for startups. Another element to consider is that occasionally intellectual property agreements are discussed too early, even before the partners understand if their business objectives are aligned and if a win–win collaboration is possible. It generally leads to a waste of time, unfocused and unproductive discussions. Intellectual property discussions tend to be difficult when the objectives of the collaboration and how strategic it is for the partners is not yet well understood.

- Establishing win–win partnerships. It is a key to developing successful collaborations, and it necessitates trust from both parties. When it involves a large corporation and a startup, due to the inequality of resources and impact the partnership has on the bottom line of the two companies, at least initially, there is sometimes a bias toward the large corporation taking a position of strength which could be detrimental to the partnership. For the large corporation, partnering with a startup brings an entrepreneurial spirit which disrupts the status quo and stimulates employees. For the startup, it provides access to resources and channels which would be otherwise difficult to access. In the startup's case, the employees need to understand the strategic importance of the collaboration as, given the scarce resources of the startup, it will clarify how to take advantage of the new capabilities.

Today, businesses, including large corporations, are disrupted daily. The pace at which new technologies and digital transformations are changing our world and the increased speed of communication changed the business landscape forever. Collaborative innovation is a must. It is driving growth and creating value, not only for the partners involved but also for consumers.

## 5.7.  THE CORPORATION-STARTUP DYNAMIC: BUILDING WIN-WIN RELATIONSHIPS

Startups adapt to live, while large corporations are somewhat less flexible and more process oriented. Startups can sometimes be hard to understand, but large corporations have to learn how to work with them, as increasingly they are becoming beneficial—even essential—for large corporations to innovate and disrupt the status quo. Of course, we are talking about two very different cultures: the large corporation—which needs to maintain its reputation, is rigorous, is policy-oriented, is more rigid with a history of taking significant challenges and being successful—and the culture of the startup, which can take more risk, is accustomed to chaos, thrives on difficult problems, is very fluid and flexible, and often is in a constant survival state. In many ways, startups and corporations are very complementary, as they have different strengths and weaknesses.

Developing a successful collaboration between a large corporation and a startup requires a strong effort in terms of expectation management. The timeframes that the two entities are used to are entirely different. While startups work in cycles of weeks or months, it is not unusual for corporations to look at years. Both sides need to understand the motives of the collaboration to ensure that both parties agree on what is achievable and when, and to avoid any misunderstanding for a win-win relationship.

While a startup can be an avenue for corporations to get involved with new technologies, corporations need to understand how they can genuinely help startups. While some startups may be looking for funding, this is often not their primary motive for seeking a collaboration. They are more interested in corporate channels and market access, customers, and resources such as technical support. By validating their product-market fit, startups are also hoping to drive up their valuation.

Besides providing access to the company resources to validate the startup technology or business model, corporations can also bring structure and processes to the collaboration. Assuming that this access does not adversely affect the collaboration speed and more generally, the partnership, it could be valuable for the startup. In the early stage, structure and processes are low on the startup priority list, as until there is a product-market fit, other things take precedence.

Making sure that the startup is talking to a decision-maker is very important, as otherwise, the startup may be spending much time explaining its operations to the corporate contact person without any tangible result. Finding the right person to talk to is often challenging as the startup has to navigate the corporate maze and get an insider perspective on people and the organizational decision process. It is also essential to understand whether or not the goals of the collaboration are in line with the corporate strategy.

While the points above play an essential role in the corporation-startup dynamic, even by paying attention to them, still in practice, many partnerships are often failing or do not produce the expected results. Some of the barriers often encountered include:

- Poor execution or overpromising from the startup company.
- The readiness of the corporation and cultural differences.
- Internal resistance from the corporate business units which may lack the resources to be involved with the startup or may want to concentrate on their current products and business models as they generally have KPIs and commitments to fulfill.
- Lack of motivation/involvement from the corporate innovation group who may feel threatened by the startup technology.
- Corporation's employees fear losing their job or the funding.
- Lack of company talent or of a champion to evaluate the benefits of the potential collaboration or push the partnership inside the corporation.

- Lack of a concrete and tangible use case that can bring focus to the collaboration project. Many corporations are looking for the startup to define a use case that fits with the corporate strategy, but this can be quite difficult as often the startup has limited information and insights about the corporation needs. Without a well-defined use case, usually, the collaboration does not progress.
- Lack of motivation for corporate employees to create a partnership due to lack of incentives. The experience shows that when the corporation has dedicated teams to take care of the collaboration with startups with clear metrics associated with it, the likelihood of success is increased.

For corporations, collaborating with startups is increasingly vital as their internal innovation teams often struggle to lead the company toward new products, services, and business models. For startups, collaborating with corporations is often a way to validate their technology or scale by leveraging the market access of the corporation. However, as discussed in this section, win-win collaborations require trust and honest communication between the different parties, a strong desire to make it work, and setting up clear expectations.

# CHAPTER 6

## Scaling and Execution

## 6.1. HOW STARTUPS CAN INNOVATE AT SCALE

Innovation is about providing new user value that you can monetize, while scaling is about repeatability and growth. A new product or service implies originality and breakthroughs, but with scaling the focus is on performance improvement, cost reduction, and automation to attract mainstream demand. The requirements for innovation and scaling are entirely different and correspond to different phases in the startup life. *Figure 6.1* highlights some of these requirements for the different innovation phases.

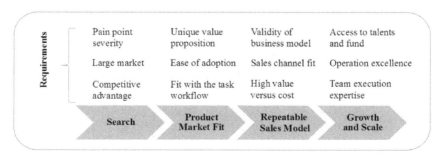

*Figure 6.1: Requirements for the different innovation phases.*

Entrepreneurs need to think about scaling when innovating. One of the significant issues for startups is that entrepreneurs often misjudge the right timing to scale because their product/service is not yet ready, the product-market fit is not proven, or they are spreading their resources too thin to do so and cannot meet the scaling requirements adequately and in a timely manner. Successful startups have scalability embedded in their mission statement, and scalability is part of everything the startup does. The velocity of scaling that is possible today was unthinkable a few years before. YouTube, as a company, was started with credit card debt. Eighteen months later it was sold to Google in an all-stock deal worth about $1.65 billion, and this is already more than a decade ago. Scaling is about having the right idea and the right mindset.

It is important not to confuse growing and scaling. As illustrated in *Figure 6.2*, growing is about adding revenues, while scaling means adding them at a much higher rate than cost, resulting in profits. Growth requires scalability, and scaling is about enabling growth. An important parameter of growth is the customer growth rate. The key to scaling is to find the processes and procedures which can move the startup toward its intended objectives.

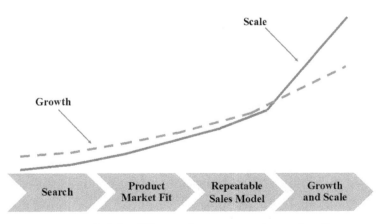

*Figure 6.2: The difference between growing and scaling.*

To be able to facilitate the scaling phase, startups have to innovate with a scaling mindset. Besides implementing policies, processes or standards at the scaling stage, startups need to always keep the big picture in mind, like designing for scale, e.g., in terms of the number of users or making sure that the platform that they are developing can expand quickly. Scaling requires focus, execution, and discipline.

Scaling is a different phase in the startup life, so it may also necessitate different leadership as it is rare that a founder can take the startup from the initial innovation phases to scaling. It can be very challenging for a startup as it is sometimes hard for an entrepreneur to relinquish the day to day operation of a startup that he/she founded and gave so much to building. For the founders, understanding their limits and bringing complementary skills into the company is often one of the keys to their success. It requires a strong foundation of respect at the highest level of the startup and a thoughtful approach to managing the transition.

Another critical point for a startup scaling its business is to move from people to process. It necessitates repeatability, velocity, and defining very clearly the schedule, roles, responsibilities, and workflows. When introducing new business functions, which is what scaling requires, creating processes that will allow people to work effectively together is not as simple as it may seem. The startup must move from individual contributions to group/team-oriented contributions. Scaling involves cross-functional teams that need to learn how to work together with well-defined interfaces between people and organizational units. Another challenge is to decide when to add a new role/responsibility. There is not one answer, and every startup is different. It is very contextual and depends on the state of the startup and where it needs to go next. It requires talent and discipline.

While communication is always crucial throughout the life of the startup, intra-company communication needs to change as a startup grows. In the early stage of the startup, a few people work closely together, usually in the same physical space, and communication is fast and informal. As the startup scales, it is often difficult to have people working in one location, and the number of people grows to a point where ad-hoc communication is not enough. At this point, creating formal communication opportunities or documenting the critical information to communicate becomes crucial, so that information propagates throughout the company for the people who should know. Establishing and enforcing procedures to accumulate and transfer knowledge is an integral part of the scaling process.

As startups grow, the members who had been involved in every decision need to delegate. It is something that many people do not find easy to do. Micromanagement must be avoided as it is not scalable, leads to employee dissatisfaction, and impacts productivity. Trust and empowerment are the solutions to overcome this. In contrast, as you hire new executives, it is important not to hire people who over-delegate (e.g., executives from large corporations accustomed to leading operations with large teams) as the startup still needs to stay nimble while it grows. For the new hires, it is about finding people who can strike the right balance between delegation and a hands-on approach.

Customization is the enemy of scale. When there is not a strong enough product-market fit, a startup spends much time customizing its solution for different customers. While in the early stage it may be necessary to provide various levels of customization to multiple customers and collect feedback, as the startup grows, it is essential to identify core capabilities that solve customer needs across many customers. Otherwise, the startup becomes a service/consultancy company, which makes scaling difficult. Standardizing feature sets and processes does not have to go against the creativity and the entrepreneurial spirit that the startup cultivated in the early stage. There are tools and approaches, enabling growth while eliminating redundancies. They aim at freeing some time by being more productive and avoiding reinventing new methods every time something new is coming up.

Scaling up to manage growth involves continuously questioning how your organization should prepare in anticipation of the intensified growth. There is a big difference between creating a few successes and building an organization for sustainable growth. This is one of the significant differences between successful startups and the ones which ride the wave without managing growth. Unfortunately, the latter often fail.

## 6.2.  SCALING STARTUPS IN CORPORATE SETTINGS

Whether the initial innovation phases start internally in a corporation, or externally from a startup that was completely independent of the corporation, one of the main challenges is scaling the business. While startups developed independently of a corporate environment have solely to win the market to be successful, startups in corporate settings have to win both the market and the "corporate mindshare" which enables the startup to operate inside the corporate environment. Therefore, though the resources provided by the corporate environment are helpful, scaling a startup in a corporate environment can be much more complicated.

While engaging with startups or empowering innovation labs to create new business is an essential activity for the corporation aiming at transforming themselves, it is not enough to innovate and validate a product-market fit. This is often the less challenging part of the new business creation. Scaling up the business and having a real business impact on the corporate bottom line is the harder part as it involves deep integration with the corporate culture, while the front-end of the business creation process which corresponds to the early phases of a startup does not require it. As illustrated in *Figure 6.3*, to create new business ventures, corporations typically use the following tools/approaches:

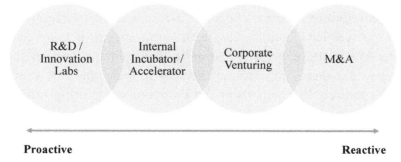

*Figure 6.3: The corporate innovation tools to create new business ventures.*

- M&A, which is usually a more reactive approach triggered by the need for speed or a complementary approach/technology to internal activities.
- Corporate venturing which often focuses on taking minority stakes into startups, giving priority to strategic alignment and cooperation.
- Internal accelerators and incubators where a corporation incubates/accelerates the startups for a while, providing them exposure to the corporate business units.
- Innovation labs, which generally focus on the front-end of the innovation process, handing out the innovation results to the business units and in rare cases creating a new business unit or spinning out a new venture outside the corporation.

In practice, all approaches have their limits. They work well when business units are engaged and take the leadership of the new business. Their main limitation lies in the creation of new business, as the existing business units tend to gravitate around their primary domain of expertise because they are also responsible for the current money-making operations. The challenge arises when a new business is a disruptive business. In this case, there is often nobody inside the corporation who can welcome this new business. Disruptive business needs a new mindset and new approaches, which are usually entirely different from the existing ones.

So how can a corporation connect its innovation front-end and back-end (responsible for scaling) so that it produces a business impact in the context of disruptive innovation opportunities? This is what corporations must try to solve. Because disruptive innovation does not yet have a home inside the corporation, it takes strong leadership at the executive corporate management level to show the way. Furthermore, because the way to scale the new venture can be entirely different from the corporation's existing business, new metrics, KPIs, and decision-making mechanisms need to be applied. The main difficulty is that the corporation needs to unlearn what worked before and approach the new business with a new mindset. Their previous success often is a barrier to doing this. One approach is to cautiously insulate the disruptive venture from the current business culture and mindset. It again necessitates support at the top executive corporate level and a clear vision to bridge the transition between the early stages of innovation and scaling. It is also essential for the new venture to grow well by not focusing only on the numbers at the expense of quality. It is something that the corporation typically knows how to do well. The likelihood of success increases if the startup can leverage the quality usually present in a corporate environment, without experiencing too much control from the corporation. One way to do this is by finding the right balance between being optimistic that the startup will reach the next level with a new approach, and pragmatism, attention to details, speed, simplicity and a quality-oriented mindset.

Corporate innovation often fails because of preconceived notions about how to scale, inertia due to an existing business that may be successful and corporate antibodies (corporate members who are afraid of change or cannot imagine how success can be different from what they did in the past). It is essential to involve corporate executives from the beginning to increase the chances of success, so that:

- They can shelter the internal startup team, and agree on the milestones.
- They grant appropriate exceptions to the corporate rules.
- They agree on the level of funding needed upon reaching the milestones.
- There is an agreement about how to execute and scale the business when the new venture reaches this point.

## 6.3. THE SECRETS OF GROWING A BUSINESS AND A SUCCESSFUL EXECUTION

Many startups have good ideas. However, many startups fail because they do not execute properly. There are many reasons why companies have problems doing so, including:

- Not clarifying roles and responsibilities.
- The lack of information flows.
- Not aligning motivators.
- An ill-formed structure.

While a superior technology, product, or business model helps to create your competitive advantage, resulting in initial traction, it is only a solid execution that will allow you to succeed in the long term. Unfortunately, many companies fail in the execution phase.

When a company wants to improve performance, very often they try to change the company structure, especially in large corporations. While shaking the current company structure can provide short-term results, this is often not sufficient if the root causes of the company's poor performance are not known. Successful execution is the result of many decisions that are performed every day by employees based on their knowledge and the information they have, their inner motivation, and their understanding of their roles and responsibilities. It is the traditional way corporations execute strategic and operational decisions. In practice, this is where things go wrong. How the information flows in the company, how people make decisions, how they are held accountable, and the clarity and relevance of the link between performance and rewards matter most. To be able to improve execution, the executive management needs to look deeply into the root causes of the company's lack of results. Often middle managers are not held accountable for their actions, or lack thereof. In a large company, it is common that a manager is moved around or promoted every few years. As they transfer to new positions frequently, they rarely see the results of their decisions and are not held accountable for them. If they do not take another job, it may be their boss who will move, resulting in a high likelihood for the directions to change. This directly impacts execution as, in such context, accountability is very weak.

To survive in today's environment and execute successfully, it is also essential to understand the relationship between performance, reward systems, motivation, and satisfaction. Reward systems, when appropriately structured and directly linked to milestones, influence employee motivation and happiness and as a consequence, performance. Rewards do not necessarily have to be monetary rewards. Recognizing or acknowledging performing employees goes a long way toward increasing motivation and satisfaction.

## 6.4. THE IMPORTANCE OF DISCIPLINED EXECUTION

Scaling innovation is not about creativity, disruption, and breakthroughs. While this is important at the beginning of the innovation process, when a startup gets to the scaling phase, it is about discipline and understanding what each employee has to do as a part of a system. It is not anymore about finding a market but rather about systematizing the growth. This is where founders struggle if they do not realize that, as the startup grows, execution and development processes, information flow and systems need to take a front stage. It is also about understanding that, as the startup grows, it is not for the founders or some key employees to solve all the problems, but instead to identify issues and find the people in the company who are best suited and qualified to address them. It can be difficult as at the initial stages of the startup it is often chaotic, and every employee assumes multiple roles.

When scaling, some startup founders fail to realize that they need their employees' impact, not just their activity or output. It is essential not to confuse motion with progress. A startup needs to create a vision of the expected result (beginning with the end in mind) that it is aiming at and empower its employees to implement processes and solutions to make this impact possible. It is about moving the responsibility and the authority to your employees instead of carrying them out as you did during the initial startup phases.

Here, is a short list of best practices, also illustrated in *Figure 6.4*, that are common to companies who are executing successfully.

- Communicate information to all key stakeholders and team members and provide them timely updates when things change. The better the communication is, the more the key stakeholders and the team will respond positively to needed changes.
- Align the strategic plan and objectives and the program execution, so that the team can focus on delivering the outcomes that meet those objectives.
- Get buy-in from the core team. It is essential to communicate effectively with the core team so that its members understand the vision behind the strategy and the objectives and are fully engaged.
- Monitor progress and performance through accountability. It is always important to follow up on any outstanding action, issue, or risk.
- Adjust for results. To keep the tasks and projects on track often necessitates some tune-up or adjusting the environment along the way.
- Acknowledge and recognize the team. As you scale, success will be dependent on the team effort. Acknowledging and sincerely giving credit to the group will ensure their engagement and help them grow with the success of your company.

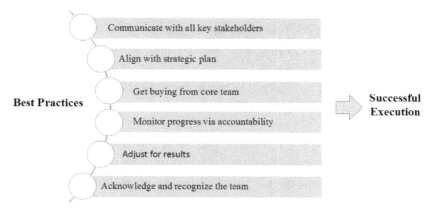

*Figure 6.4: Best practices for successful execution.*

Disciplined execution is vital when expanding a startup into its next phase of growth (McChesney, Covey, & Huling, 2012). If there is not enough discipline, there is no consistency, which is essential for priorities, metrics, communication, and generally for the business. During scaling, the focus is on managing people, following processes, and communicating information effectively to all the stakeholders, sponsors, and team members. It is a significant departure from the initial unpredictable and chaotic phases of a startup and often necessitates the hiring of new employees who have done this before and can put the necessary processes in place.

## 6.5. PUTTING IN PLACE THE RIGHT STRUCTURE TO SCALE INNOVATION

Corporations have a pyramidal structure which is not prone to risk-taking as the middle-level managers often stop innovation because they do not have the vision to carry it forward or they do not have incentives to try something new. One possible solution is to change the structure through which new ideas and business opportunities are evaluated and approved. For a startup in the scaling phase, it is essential to be mindful of this risk and to continually search and innovate the company structure to improve the company effectiveness.

As the startup grows, there is a risk of inertia so, similar to the product/service development level, the startup should be willing to experiment with designing the organizational structure that will be the most efficient. *Figure 6.5* shows some tips/advice that can help startups figure out how to put in place the right framework for them. Below are more details about these tips.

- Avoid creating silos. Instead, build multidisciplinary teams that collaborate, as active collaboration is a crucial ingredient to the company success. By organizing activities into small groups which have some autonomy, it is possible to decide in a decentralized way and to create speed.

- Lead through the culture. When the company grows, it is harder to move quickly and to move the whole organization in the same direction. By creating a culture and a mindset valuing innovation, speed, and calculated risk-taking, the growing company can empower its employees to continue to innovate without sitting on ideas and increasing bureaucracy. Creating a culture of autonomy and accountability goes a long way toward sustaining innovation and being agile enough to adapt and scale successfully.

- Create a bias toward actions and responsibility. A consensus-based culture is slow and is not responsive enough. By being accountable for what you do, and understanding the results of what you do, you can learn from failures and obtain useful information that will allow you to improve.

- Constantly innovate your organizational structure. Building the organizational structure is a design experiment. Entrepreneurs should always be rethinking the optimum organization that can yield the maximum efficiency while continuing to innovate. As the company grows, the organization should evolve. How to foster collaboration and execution speed should be one of the metrics. The executive team should be willing to experiment while progressing toward this goal.

- Constantly re-evaluate and re-design your processes. Continuously creating new means that bring people together and encourage collaboration is essential, and an iterative mindset is often the right approach. Even if a project does not meet the objectives set at the starting phase, it still provides useful information and valuable lessons. Ingraining this iteration and continuous improvement mindset inside the organization is a way to evolve the organization continuously.
- Look for champions/catalysts. Not everybody inside an organization has the capabilities to lead and innovate. Thus, as the company scales and grows, it is crucial to identify champions within the organization who can expand innovation throughout the entire organization.

*Figure 6.5: Tips and advice to put in place the right structure for successful execution.*

As the company scales, it is essential to combine disciplined execution with a flexible structure allowing small teams to make decisions in a decentralized way. This is one of the challenges that scaling brings to the growing startup. It is essential to have processes to increase revenues and at the same time, to innovate toward what will be needed to compete and be successful in the future.

## 6.6. STARTING IN EUROPE/ASIA AND SCALING IN THE UNITED STATES

For many startups who began their journey outside the United States, as they expand, they are often asking themselves about entering the United States market. Growing and scaling their business in the United States makes a better story and in general, gives them access to a higher valuation than in Europe or Asia. They also can have better access to capital as compared to other countries. In Europe or Asia, startups get financial support for the initial phases of startup life via mechanisms such as government grants, local assistance, or national projects. However, as they get some traction and want to raise Series A funds, it becomes more difficult as there is less appetite for risk as compared, for example, to Silicon Valley in the United States. The size of investments is also usually much more significant in the United States as compared to Europe or Asia.

Another reason why a startup can be interested in scaling in the United States is that the United States has a sizeable homogeneous market as compared to other countries. In Europe, for example, to reach a similar population, the startup will have to deal with many languages and a fair amount of localization effort (e.g., marketing, taxes, shipping) which can be very complicated and expensive. However, it is also essential to understand that the United States can be quite a different market than the home market as good performance at a low cost, convenience, and a great user experience are generally necessary for the products/services that are accepted by the United States market. It is also a very complex and highly competitive market.

The United States market is well known to be better suited for exits, as compared to other countries in the world. While many counties are doing a great job at encouraging entrepreneurs in their journey and supporting them along the way, it is still striking to see the low number of exits as compared to the number of startups present in their ecosystem. Large corporations often acquire startups to enter into some new fields or boost their competency. However, for example, in

Europe, there are not many large companies who could spend millions of euros on acquisitions, and it is also not part of their strategy. In the United States, it is more common, especially for technology companies such as Apple, Facebook, Google, or Microsoft.

A strategy often adopted by Asian and European companies is to start in their home country and to expand to the United States via business development activities, while leaving the engineering workforce in their home country. It can provide several benefits as their home country may yield a cost advantage. It may also be easier to recruit talent as compared to some regions in the United States, like Silicon Valley where new hires are expensive, and it is difficult to compete with large technology companies that provide large salaries and attractive benefits. It also allows startups to prove their product/service in their home country and achieve a product-market fit in a market that they understand, that is likely less complex than a foreign one, and then to scale their business in the United States.

Though it is difficult to generalize, one of the significant differences between the European/Asian and the United States startups is that in Europe and Asia one of the objectives is often to be profitable, while in the United States and especially in Silicon Valley it is all about scaling and growing fast. In Europe and Asia, startups tend to get support from grants and their respective local and national governments. This help can continue for some time, allowing the startup to get some traction and sometimes to be profitable, but there is not this urge to expand quickly. In Europe and Asia, it is not uncommon to find a startup that has been in business for ten years with revenues that allow them barely to survive. In the United States, this is very rare as non-growing startups will not raise their next round of funding. It enables pushing toward the top the most promising startups, while in Europe and Asia startups tend to survive for a long time, diluting somewhat the startup ecosystem and making it more challenging to separate the good startups from the other ones. When a startup with a mindset of being profitable comes to the United States and tries to scale, it is often quite hard as they usually do not take the level of risk necessary to expand quickly making it difficult to attract funding from investors.

Finally, one more element to consider that may not always be in favor of starting a new business in your home country is the interpretation of failures. In some societies, when you fail, it is difficult to start a new venture, as it will be difficult to be credible again or to obtain a line of credit, while in the United States failure is often synonymous with experience and is not viewed negatively. Failure brings learning and prepares you for your next endeavor. All the points above are essential to decide where to start your new venture and what the best strategy is in order to scale.

## 6.7.  CLOSING THE PLAN/STRATEGY-EXECUTION GAP

Many companies, especially large companies, are still following a "Plan-then-Do" approach. Much time is spent on planning, making sure that the direction is right and that there is a good understanding of the competitive landscape before initiating the execution phase. Not surprisingly, the results often fall short of expectations. It is because there is no room for experimentation and adaptation, which is necessary for today's fast-paced changes. Also, a plan is still a guess and, following market feedback, the assumption may prove to be wrong, or at least not optimal.

In today's software world of continuous refinement and rapid iterations, it is wiser to adopt a "hypothesis-validation" approach instead of mid-to-long-term planning followed by execution. The focus should be on near-term decisions with a long-term vision. It is about the recognition that there is not only one path toward the goal, but instead a journey that is made of constant learning and adaptation to find the best way forward. It is a continuous process instead of being a sequential and batch approach toward reaching the goals. One of the requirements of this process is flexibility, and in today's ever-increasing speed of change, flexibility matters.

In a world where mega-corporations face disruption in a matter of months instead of years, it is essential to adjust course to be able to deal with the unexpected. It requires building a fast-paced organization able to learn and react quickly but also a strategy built on a portfolio of opportunities which will allow emphasizing some directions at the expense of others based on real-time learning. It is something often difficult to implement for large companies that have been used to moving based on certainty instead of dealing with the uncertainty inherent in today's world. One of the keys to doing this is to use the portfolio approach to be ready to go into a particular direction and to increase the effort and investment when the conditions are right and more evidence is obtained.

If we look at how companies are making decisions, still too much emphasis is put on their past experiences. While past experiences, successes, and failures are valuable reference points, it is essential to keep an open mind and not to let past experiences unconditionally lead how we see the world forward. Unlearning from past experiences and being open to how the world can be different enables out-of-the-box thinking, which is necessary to drive change. An approach to do this, while progressing with an uncertain view of the future, is to articulate hypotheses, to test them, to learn from the experiments and to iterate. It is the concept of agile planning, which allows one to define and refine a strategy before spending too much time executing it and potentially wasting much money. Most large companies do not take advantage of this methodology or do not know how to modify their organization to enable it. To obtain great results requires a great strategy and excellent execution. However, many companies need a new approach to strategy and execution, which involves a constant interaction between the two until collected evidence validates the execution plan. This process allows closing the strategy-execution gap, which is one of the main reasons promising companies fail.

## 6.8. SCALING BY LEVERAGING SUPPLIERS

A company is only as good as its supply chain. As companies look to compete globally, supply chain effectiveness becomes a key differentiator, as demonstrated by Apple significantly driving down expenses while improving lead times considerably (Cordon & Nie, 2011). *Figure 6.6* highlights some of the essential characteristics of effective supply chain management. The fast pace of going to market makes agility a must. Companies need to be able to scale up and down the supply chain quickly to be competitive. The supply chain is getting digitalized and disrupted. By using technologies like blockchain (Norman, 2017), the supply chain complexity is decreasing, thanks to automation. Platforms are progressively providing a seamless integration between buyers and their supply chain partners where you connect once to the platform, and you can collaborate with all partners.

Companies need to understand the value stack and where to provide value. Designing your product or service so that it integrates smoothly in the value stack will allow you to focus only on your core value. An examination of how your value-add areas will position your company to optimize the entire supply chain more efficiently will allow you to increase your overall value offering considerably.

Many companies are prioritizing cost-reduction over flexibility, but this is not always the best. An agile supply chain that can quickly adjust to changes in supply and demand can be critical. Also connecting your customers to your supply chain (e.g., via tracking information, delivery notifications) can go a long way into improving the user experience.

*Figure 6.6: Leveraging the suppliers and the supply
chain as a source of competitive advantage.*

The supply chain and the technologies that are progressively integrating with the supply chain can enable you to scale effectively and could turn into a compelling advantage. A best-in-class supply chain will allow you to save money, have more efficient operations, and make better decisions.

## 6.9.  GROWING VIA M&A AND AN ACQUISITION STRATEGY

For many large corporations, traditional R&D has been failing at creating new business opportunities, and many companies have been looking at various acquisition strategies such as M&A as a way to drive growth and innovation. As shown in *Figure 6.7*, acquisitions can be in the form of purchasing assets such as IP, taking minority stakes in other companies or full acquisition known as M&A. In this section, we will focus mainly on M&A.

Many companies struggled to use M&A effectively. The ones who succeed are developing a long-term strategy that incorporates a good understanding of the role of M&A in executing it. An excellent example is Google's acquisition of Android in 2005 for $50 million. At the time it was a small acquisition. However, Google saw this acquisition as a significant step forward toward a growth initiative in the smartphone market. When coupled with a long-term strategy, venture acquisitions can be an effective and efficient way to achieve company targets versus an organic expansion. The success post-acquisition depends on careful strategic planning pre-acquisition. There needs to be a strategic fit between the two companies and a certain level of organizational and cultural fit. When acquisitions aim at short-term synergies and not transformational growth, their impact tends to be more limited as it becomes an annual budget exercise often challenging to sustain. Furthermore, the short-range focus drives up acquisition costs due to the competition.

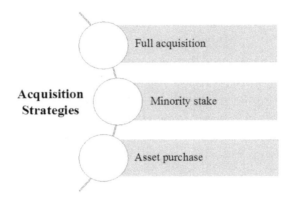

*Figure 6.7: Acquisition strategies.*

Most companies who are considering an acquisition strategy have at least one of the following motivations:

- Lack of internal innovation to be able to compete.
- A surplus of cash and a shortage of ideas to use it profitably.
- A need to evolve in-house capabilities.
- A need to support their core business (e.g., via IP acquisition).
- Financial merit.
- A goal to enter a new business accelerated through an acquisition strategy.
- A purpose to remove competition.

In all cases for the M&A to be successful, it is essential to make sure that it aligns with the company's long-term strategic objectives, that the right leaders are available to execute the integration and that it drives value by balancing short-term tactical goals with long-term strategic ones.

According to a KPMG study published on January 27, 2015, 83% of the mergers fail and do not boost shareholder returns. Some of the reasons often brought forward include mismanagement of risk, price, strategy, cultures, and management capacity. One of the common failures is not to have a clear integration plan and to underestimate the importance of planning the first 100 days very carefully as they are crucial for successful integration. Additional difficulties that an M&A can bring include:

- Lack of or unclear communication. Especially in the initial phases of the merger, people are looking for clear guidance and action. Addressing people's concerns and communicating with employees, empowering them, and creating a culture for them to thrive in are all fundamental parts of the integration.
- Cultural motivations. It is always a challenge during a merger to adopt another company culture. During a merger, changes are happening in management practices, strategies, processes, communications, and these changes can have a negative impact on some of the people inside the organization.
- Employee retention. A merger can bring uncertainty about job security, role changes, and lead to stress and anxiety impacting employees and their future in the organization. It is critical to explain the benefits of the merger and to work toward boosting employee morale so as to maintain or regain talented employees' trust so that they do not look for other companies.
- Overestimating the synergies. Synergies include the following areas: cross-selling to the customers of the two companies, economies of scale due to the enhanced combined power, and savings from combining the two companies' hopefully

complementary activities (e.g., sales, administration). While synergies may be attractive in theory, it is not uncommon for the synergies to be less than expected. Creating and thoroughly validating a financial model before the merger helps to minimize the risks.

- Not making the tough decisions. When the integration takes place, you may realize that there is redundancy between the two companies, that some of the people are not appropriate to help your next level of growth or that the integration of the teams is more complicated than planned. If that is the case, experience shows that it is best to resolve integration issues quickly instead of postponing decisions, even if some of these decisions may be tough to make.

If we look at the most successful firms in the world (e.g., Apple, Facebook, Google), all of them rely on acquisition to achieve their strategic goals. It is often the faster way to go into some new areas or achieve targets as compared to organic expansion. However, as discussed above, having a long-term strategy is generally one of the keys for an acquisition to create a significant impact.

# CHAPTER 7

## Going Global

### 7.1.  WHY GO GLOBAL?

Startups can expand vertically, by focusing on their market niche or geography, and they can grow horizontally, by venturing into new countries or new areas of business. The beachhead or home market typically provides the startup their initial customers or "early adopters," followed by their "early majority" customers, if the startup can successfully establish a product-market fit. One of the next stages of the startup evolution is an expansion into international markets (Gioeli, 2014).

The above has been the typical startup trajectory. However, in recent years with the pace of change accelerating and the ability to access other markets more easily via modern communications (e.g., Internet communication such as video conference), automation (requiring fewer resources) and global platforms (e.g., global accelerators), international expansion tends to happen much quicker.

This accelerating pace to access global markets has some positives and negatives. On the one hand, as the Internet has changed the limitations of geographical boundaries, it is easier for startups to find new customers abroad, e.g., with large markets such as the United States, and large emerging markets such as China or India which can offer scale. On the other hand, startups are not always well prepared to deal with the complexity of going global or may be tempted too early to go global without having validated the product/service sufficiently in their beachhead market. It is often the case of startups founded in small European countries or the like. Reasons for startups to go global include the following points:

- New revenue potential by expanding their markets and, as a consequence, their customer base.
- Reduction of dependence on their current markets to spread out the risk.
- Specific characteristics of the new markets that they are targeting, which may be suitable to their offering.
- Expansion of the sales life of their current products.
- Advantages in terms of investment or other tangible benefits which necessitate a presence in the target markets.
- Greater access to talents.

Technology and the predominance of software products have been a major driving force connecting different markets. Online services do not have boundaries and can spread quickly in many new markets. Startups are leveraging technology's capabilities to create a global market for their offering. Global expansion can provide several advantages. However, it does not come without challenges. Before doing so, it is essential to create an effective strategy that will allow your startup to go over the hurdles of globalization and to enjoy the rewards. The following sections provide more details.

## 7.2.  WHAT TO DO BEFORE GOING GLOBAL?

Having traction in your home market doesn't guarantee success in foreign markets. So, if you have in mind to expand internationally, it is best not to rush, and to give yourself time to perform the necessary due diligence, to conduct the required research, to seek trusted counsel and to develop a strategy. Hereafter are some tips which are useful to follow before getting started in a foreign country.

- Choose your new market(s). You may wonder, "How do I choose the right markets?" Moreover, "How many countries can I enter at once?" Many businesses enter foreign markets because they come across an opportunity or a new potential customer (opportunistic approach), or because they did a market analysis and gathered some market intelligence. Often it is a combination of both.
- Understand the country's political climate. You do not want to be in a position where your profits are unexpectedly taxed, and you do not want to risk your assets because of an unstable political or economic system. Understanding these points is essential.
- Research business practices (e.g., banking, taxation, country laws, and legal requirements). By being aware of the business rules, taxations, and needs to do business in a foreign country, you will be in a position to plan for it and avoid disagreeable surprises.
- Seek legal advice. You do not need to reinvent the wheel. It is generally a good practice to hire a lawyer or retain the services of a law firm who will be able to give you advice about what you should do and should avoid.
- Understand the market. Each market is different, and what works in your home country may not work in your new market. To avoid any bad surprise, you should experiment with your target market and gather evidence to validate your product-market fit again. A market like the United States is very cost sensitive, and customers require a high degree

of convenience, along with an excellent user experience. Customers in Europe or Japan tend to focus more on quality and less on price.

- Be familiar with cultural differences and understand how they may affect your business. You can prepare by spending some time in your target market or hire a local expert who could guide you to understand local traditions, customs, and business practices, how they could influence your sales and marketing efforts and how to fit in your new market business community.

- Develop an entry strategy. There are many different ways to enter a market. You may want to hire local talents, transfer people from your home office, or partner with a local company who already has expertise in the new market. All solutions have pros and cons. You also need to determine the best channels to enter the market as they may be different from the ones you used in your home market. Careful planning and experimentation will be necessary.

- Understand local compliance. You need to understand what is required to do business in your target market. Do you need to have your product certified in your target market to be able to do business? Global regulations (e.g., packing regulations and recycling rules) are always evolving, so you need to pay attention to them and work with advisors so that you understand how this is impacting your business.

- Understand the competition. You need to know how crowded your target market is, and your unique value proposition as compared to competitors in your target market. It will allow you to position your product effectively and launch a good marketing campaign.

- Hire appropriately and progressively after validating your hypotheses about your target market. Initially, it is often a good idea to rely on experts in your target market, even if it is on a contractual or part-time basis so that you can quickly get a feel for the market and validate your hypotheses. You can follow with a more aggressive approach to hiring after having eliminated some of the risks. With local employees, you can bridge cultural and language barriers.

While the list above is not exhaustive, these points help to decrease the uncertainties associated with expanding into a new market, while reducing the risks of failure. Growing your business via new international markets can be rewarding, but also risky if you are not well prepared. You should first make sure that you have a good product-market fit and traction in your home market, before expanding into new markets. Global expansion can be a necessary step to increase your revenues and reach more customers, but it will also increase the complexity of your business. In this case, you should ask yourself: "Do I want to do this? Is my company ready?" While going global sounds exciting, it also requires patience, a strong value proposition, and the desire to learn about new markets, before reaping the benefits of the expansion.

## 7.3. SOME OFTEN UNDERESTIMATED CHALLENGES TO EXPANDING BUSINESS GLOBALLY

While many companies incorporate in their strategic plan the intention of globalizing their organization, only a small number have the execution capabilities needed to implement it successfully. Often they may need to start all over again to be successful away from their home market. Though they may have a product/service to start, in the new markets they have no traction and no customers, no relationship and no partner and little experience about the business environment and local culture. Among the challenges encountered, it is common to underestimate the ones below.

- The go-to-market, logistics, and other value chain activities which are sometimes not carefully considered. A product/service offering is necessary, but it is only one small part of what it takes to be successful. How to reach and acquire customers, how to deliver products to them at a reasonable cost and how to support them when they have issues all need to be deeply understood and worked out to the satisfaction of the company customers. It is not simple! It is also worth noting the difference between hardware and software/service products. The dynamics of warranty replacement and repair for physical productions create unique capability needs and logistics.

- The impact of time zones can be huge and can negatively impact the communication between team members residing in different countries, as well as timely support to customers. As an example, if some members of the team live on the United States West Coast and need to communicate with other members leaving in Europe, they have to deal with a time difference of eight or nine hours. It limits communication time significantly during regular business hours. It also weighs heavily on support windows (e.g., 12-hour call center versus 24/7 operations).

- To support a global agenda, a company has to align the organization. It can be difficult as it is easy to ignore issues or challenges happening in markets which are far away from you. Often the company HQ is optimistic and does not have a sense of urgency when they are far away from the new markets' day-to-day operation.

- Local managers need to be fully committed to the success of the organization, as they are the ears and eyes on the ground. They also need to be able to play an essential role in defining the strategy of the company for their local markets instead of only providing inputs to the company HQ. Product/service localization can also be time-consuming and costly. It is something to consider carefully.

- When working internationally, finances and pricing become a little more complicated. Exchange rates are very dynamic, but the price list cannot change all the time. The company needs to be able to consider these variations without being priced out of the market because it is not competitive. Tax rules also need to be understood thoroughly. It often necessitates some local support.

- An adaptation to the market space is necessary. In the United States, the business world moves quickly, and when people have issues, they want to have a quick resolution. This is not always the case in other countries where people may have a clear separation between their personal and professional life resulting in tolerated delays or a different sense of urgency.

- Having local partners on the ground is essential. There are many ways to do this, such as contractual arrangements, temporary assignments, or even via volunteers. In a place like Silicon Valley, which has a pay forward culture, it is not too difficult to find people with experience who are willing to help you. It highlights the power of finding people who have a strong network. Depending on the problems you are coming across, they can help you connect to people that can assist you.

Different cultural norms and customer needs in the markets you are targeting may require you to adjust your marketing/sales approach or even your full offering. Before making some decisions, you need to think about how your customers will receive them and how they will be affected. While the company should stay true to its brand, finding the right balance between incorporating many local requirements and running a fast and scalable operation is critical.

## 7.4. POSSIBLE STRATEGIES TO TAKE YOUR COMPANY GLOBAL

Besides the United States, the natural new market opportunities are Canada, Mexico, Europe, Japan, South Korea, China, and India, due to their economies, or large populations. However, this is only a very shallow view of where the path to expanding lies as there are many other fast-growing, less-competitive markets. There are many strategies to consider that may be better suited to the stage your startup is at and the value proposition you are offering. It includes some of the ones below.

- It is essential to choose the most suitable market (or markets) for your startup, and it may not necessarily be the biggest market. It should be the most relevant according to the product/service you are offering, the relationships you may have, or the help that you can get in the targeted markets. Some markets are also more prone to rapid growth, some are less competitive, and some are more culturally ready than others.

- It is wise to choose your market based on your understanding of customer habits and cultural norms in the selected market to assess the suitability of your product or service, to learn how much you need to adapt to the local environment, and to determine whether it is worth targeting that market. You need to understand both the local and global implications of your decisions.

- It can be an excellent strategy to choose a global acceleration platform or location as a springboard to go global. In the United States, Silicon Valley is an important location as many global companies have an office in the region, and people in Silicon Valley do not care about the origin of your company. It makes it easier to grow and develop, raise funds, and access global companies and programs that will help you go global. It also hosts some innovation ecosystems such as Plug and Play, a Silicon Valley-based startup accelerator, which are helpful in accelerating the creation of global businesses. Plug and Play provides an innovation environment matching global corporations with global startups. It has offices and programs in quite a few countries, making it easy to link innovation capabilities from several countries.

- Paying attention to how individual behaviors and attitudes (micro level) interact with the social environment (macro level) provides some cues toward potential opportunities. A macro perspective is often not enough, as it does not go deep enough into culture, attitude, and behaviors. Understanding this interaction can also allow for discovering some barriers to adoption, as was the case for Uber who found that their platform to sign up drivers was not working in Egypt because of social values and cultural understanding of the English language and digital platforms.

- Think deeply about your go-to-market strategy and how you will distribute and support your products from opening a company-owned subsidiary to partnering with distributors or setting up joint ventures. Whatever you choose, combining local insights and expertise with a global understanding of the macro context will be essential to being successful.

There is not a silver bullet to be successful, and many companies try some directions and then adapt according to what they learn. The most successful companies are the ones who stay agile. You need to find the solution that works for you and is a good fit with your context, product/service, financial resources, and situation.

## 7.5. THREE TIPS THAT WILL CONTRIBUTE TO YOUR SUCCESS WHEN EXPANDING GLOBALLY

As you grow and scale across new markets, you will confront a new set of challenges and while growth is exciting, the stress that it creates can take a toll on an entrepreneur who is looking into new market opportunities. Three tips are helpful when expanding to new markets to help you navigate these challenges. They are summarized in *Figure 7.1* and below.

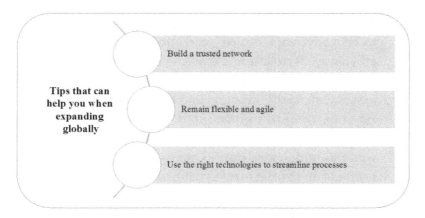

*Figure 7.1: Useful tips when expanding globally.*

- You will need to grow your network, your relationships, your list of suppliers and vendors and hire new employees to help you carry out your expansion. These relationships will require a high level of trust and making mistakes in this area can set you back significantly or even put your business in danger. People and trusted connections can be your greatest assets as they will help you identify opportunities and advocate your growth along the way. If you are opening an office in a new country, the manager of the new office should be someone whom you can trust and who already knows your company and culture well. Opening a new office necessitates many adaptations between your company's norms and the local environment. The new office needs to be an extension of your company, and it starts with the person leading it. Scaling the company is only achievable via the building of a trusted network that will allow you to bring your company to the next level as you cannot do it alone.

- To expand, as discussed in the previous sections, you need to establish a clear vision and strategy to achieve your goals. While it is good to have a plan, it is essential to remain flexible and agile, and each market that you approach will bring you discoveries and a whole new set of learning. I have seen too many startups who want to scale trying to execute an expansion strategy based on the knowledge that they have in their own country. Initially, maintaining a light and agile footprint while focusing on learning allows startups to take advantage of new market opportunities quickly and efficiently. Remaining flexible when testing new markets before making a permanent long-term commitment is the best way to justify expenses and ensure a long-term ROI.

- As your company grows, it is essential to use the right technologies to help you streamline processes. It can include communication mechanisms, management systems, customer relationship management systems, and personal productivity applications. Cloud-based collaboration tools make it very easy to share documents and business leads and keep everybody on the same page—if they are kept up to date. Automation and early definition of clear interfaces will help to avoid miscommunications and create decision-making speed even when people are remote.

The tips above may seem obvious. However, an entrepreneur has many things to worry about, and it is easy to forget something. Keeping them in mind when you grow can set the right foundation, enabling your success.

## 7.6.  PRODUCT/SERVICE LOCALIZATION

Previously, products were mass produced and then sold globally. With the transition from products to services, the growing power of software and the era of digital transformation, market customization and localization is becoming more and more critical. As you progressively understand the new markets, you want to come up with a localization strategy. You need to understand what it takes to localize your products/services, from language localization to product features and marketing effort. According to your limited resources and the business you are in, what are the languages and areas that you need to prioritize? One of the big questions to answer is what the content strategy should be, in other words, the marketing, and product-related content. Most of your content should fit into these buckets: branding and identity, website, marketing material, brand communication, support documentation, installation manuals, blogs, social media, and legal documents such as service agreements. Initially, not everything might be required to start doing business, but they will progressively become necessary.

Besides content, it will be essential to assess how your product/service needs to be modified to fit with the new market's local environment. It is a tougher call and often requires some collaboration with local experts as by default, we tend to judge a market based on the knowledge we have of other ones. Some markets, like the United

States, emphasize convenience and cost, while other markets, such as East Asian markets, emphasize quality and design and are willing to pay a premium. A startup often cannot afford to localize product/ service features extensively. However, some level of adaptation may be needed to consider local preferences and critical factors. As always, there will be a balance between maintaining your global brand, localizing, the resources that you have available, and managing the complexity which comes with localization.

Once you set a strategy and execute it, you want to measure the impact of your localization and market expansion continuously. You should always evaluate if your plan is working, if you should change direction, or if you want to continue down this path. To do this, you want to carefully watch some indicators that will tell you if you are going in the right direction or not (e.g., the effectiveness of your website to bring new customers, how your marketing outreach is working). These indicators will help you determine if your investment yields the desired results that you envisioned.

## 7.7. MANAGING CULTURAL DIFFERENCES AND THE IMPORTANCE OF CULTURE

The companies that can think globally have a competitive edge (Jensen, 2017). However, even with the most brilliant global strategy and business vision, if companies do not pay attention to the social and cultural elements of doing business in a foreign country, the chances of failure are high. When you work globally, it is essential to pay attention to cultural etiquette, commonly defined as the codes of behavior that rule different cultures. The challenge is that there is not one uniform set of standards around the globe. For example, a hand gesture in one country may have the exact opposite meaning in another culture. In some cultures (such as in Korea and Japan), there is an expectation that employees must defer to their managers. This deference is often a reason why it is hard to get honest feedback during meetings.

As you expand internationally, the critical element of a successful business outcome may be the respect and appreciation of cultural differences. It will be essential for you to learn about cultural differences and to utilize your knowledge of cultural diversity to be successful. A piece of advice often mentioned is to focus, at least initially, 80% on the relationship and 20% on the deal. It is also essential not to be too aggressive at the beginning of a relationship. Americans have a reputation of getting things done and sometimes of being too aggressive. You need to be sensitive to how the other party feels, and it is always wise to put the relationship first, not the deal. If you are aware of particular distinctions between cultures and you show respect for them, the people you are dealing with will feel respected, will appreciate it and this will help your business. Often, finding common ground is sufficient, and it is not necessary to abide by all the cultural differences.

In almost any business these days, you will have to interact with people from a different cultural background than yours. You may have colleagues from a different country, or you may partner with organizations whose employees are from a different country. Some of your customers may have a different cultural origin. When it comes to cultural differences, the goal is to understand the needs of the other person and to communicate at a deeper level. In other words, it is to figure out what the motivators are for that culture versus the motivators for yours.

Global companies tend to hire local managers who understand their business and the local culture to deal with cultural differences. It helps to create a bridge between company management and local employees. However, this does not solve all the issues as the company cannot ignore its global identity, processes, and culture at the expense of abiding by the local culture. You need to find a balance without sacrificing the company values. Best Buy is an interesting example, as it closed its branches in China for failing to differentiate its products from that of competitors, and for not adapting to local consumers' shopping preferences.

Working successfully with cultural diversity requires understanding different social behaviors, especially those that are less obvious and that we take for granted. One of these is implicit communication, which is common in informal situations. During international company expansion, such informal communication methods stop working, as the implicit part of the communication is lost; this can be a great source of misunderstanding and inefficiency when people are living in different parts of the world.

Dealing with cultural differences requires time, patience, and an understanding that deals can take time to materialize. In the United States, people tend to get frustrated if they do not hear from you in a few days, while in countries like Japan, it may take weeks because the decision process is consensus-based. It is a striking difference between United States and most Asian cultures. In the United States, we equate time with money, and if you are not early, you are late. For most Asian cultures, things happen when they are supposed to, and time is more flexible and elastic. Asian cultures have a long-term orientation.

In today's world, companies who want to be successful need to succeed in the global economy and leverage the power of culture to optimize the company's bottom line. Cross-cultural differences are often cited as the most significant barriers to expand internationally. On the other hand, the companies who can incorporate a cross-cultural framework into their operations have a definite competitive advantage.

## 7.8. THE BIGGEST CHALLENGES OF EXPANDING IN THE ASIA PACIFIC MARKETS SUCH AS CHINA AND JAPAN

The Asia Pacific is no longer just a place where companies outsource manufacturing and customer support, but also an essential area for developing new markets. For example, a market like China is booming with an average annual growth of 10% over the past 30 years, and Japan is an innovative market which is a great retail laboratory for many luxury brands and companies who want to improve the quality of their products. However, Chinese and Japanese business cultures are very different from what we are accustomed to in the United States. It is crucial to understand the challenges you will face on your path to thrive in these countries.

Markets like China and Japan are transitioning from manufacturing to services and consumer-based consumption. They have a definite appetite for technology, high-end consumer items, and infrastructure. China has a booming e-commerce industry, and market liberalization of critical sectors such as finance and telecom drove its growth. However, to be successful in these countries, it is essential to tailor your business behavior, communication, and personal branding to these market audiences. For example, American and Western European cultures focus on the individual. East Asian cultures focus more on the group, valuing the needs of the group over the needs of the individual. American civilian person-to-person relationships tend to be quite flat. In contrast, East Asian relationships are more hierarchical, and most of the time, behaviors are dictated by who is present in the room.

With markets like China and Japan, it is essential to be patient as credibility and trust need time. It is also crucial to be present in these markets regularly as these markets emphasize face-to-face communication and relationship building. Finally, it is essential to see things from this market viewpoint and to tailor behavior, communication, and personal branding to the target audience. Because Japan and China have a strong background in manufacturing and hardware, it is essential to be tangible and concrete instead of abstract and vague. Being on time and meeting deadlines is vital to building trust and being viewed as a reliable partner. Failure to understand simple but subtle issues in communication and business behaviors may damage your reputation, which is devastating to the business relationship and often unrecoverable.

When meeting with Chinese or Japanese business counterparts, you want to set an agenda in advance and send any relevant documents before your meeting. It is also good to confirm what you want to talk about or what you want to achieve before starting the discussion. Gift giving is essential for the development of goodwill and trust, and business rarely stops when the meeting is over. Entertainment and dining play a crucial role in relationship building and in "learning" about each other.

Western style of communication is direct, while in East Asian cultures, communication is very subtle and indirect. Even with the best intentions, a direct communication style can create a significant offense. In Japan, for example, the word "no" is rarely used, and an indirect form of communication is preferred. Failures to understand this can be a waste of time and money and jeopardize business opportunities.

The above represent some well-known challenges often encountered when doing business in the Asia Pacific markets. They constitute some of the roadblocks of doing business. You should also be aware of the following additional potential difficulties:

- In the West, many administrative tasks are now more straightforward, though sometimes underappreciated. In the Asia Pacific, administration and bureaucratic tasks, such as opening a bank account or registering your company, can be time-consuming. You need to be ready.
- Western employees tend to delegate responsibility and have flexible lines of authority. This is generally not the case in East Asian cultures where there is a more hierarchical structure, and everybody tends to have a distinct role. Decisions often necessitate a consensus-building approach which takes time.
- In the United States, startups tend to be mission-driven (especially in Silicon Valley) with a novel idea or a definite purpose to impact the industry in a particular way, while in China, for example, startups are mainly market-driven

with the primary objective to make much money. The core motivation of Chinese entrepreneurs is to generate financial gain and to get rich. Because of this, Chinese entrepreneurs are more willing to experiment and change their execution strategy, if this means increased profits.

- Given the complexity of the Asia Pacific markets, traditional methods of gathering business intelligence such as surveys, or focus groups, are not sufficient. It is essential to be present in these markets to better understand customers from these markets. It can be a valuable competitive advantage.

The Asia Pacific, including China and Japan taken as examples in this section, is a significant source of services and technologies. China is progressively becoming a superpower in the area of Artificial Intelligence. As the middle class in these countries is becoming wealthier, the Asia Pacific is a potential that is often untapped. It is something that many growing companies cannot ignore. However, to be able to compete and enter these markets successfully, it is essential to understand these markets' customers and business practices deeply.

# CHAPTER 8

## The Corporation Challenges

## 8.1. CREATING A CULTURE OF INNOVATION

Corporations are optimized for efficiency, processes, and certainty. It is one of the main reasons why new business creation is much harder in large companies than in startups. The image for corporate innovation is to belong to one department (often called R&D) of the organizational structure, which is managed the same way as the other corporate departments. This is the crux of the problem. Innovation requires the building of an innovation culture, which makes it safe to make mistakes and learn. When the emphasis is on efficiency and certainty via corporate planning, there is a high probability that innovation will die.

Creating a corporate innovation culture is not easy as it requires a different mindset from the one needed to execute the current business. It is about enabling a set of behaviors that empower people to experiment and unleash their curiosity. Organization leaders who celebrate learning—even if it is from mistakes—shape this culture and practice it during the day-to-day operations. Empowering people to change the status quo requires the elimination of the fear of failure. The organizations which are successful in doing this provide *psychological safety*—this means a climate in which individuals feel that they can speak truthfully and openly, without fear of reprisal.

*Figure 8.1* summarizes some of the essential characteristics found in companies that have enabled a culture of innovation. Amazon and Google, in different ways, are two examples. The Amazon way is to be customer-centric and customer-obsessed. At Amazon, everything starts with the customer and works backward from there. Before working on a new product, it always begins by writing a press release to lay out details about the customer benefits and what value is provided. Amazon favors small teams, often called "two-pizza teams" as they should not be too large and should not require more than two pizzas to feed the group. These project teams take full ownership of the projects from the beginning. At Amazon, there is an understanding that taking some risk is OK, and that not everything will succeed. It is fine as long as the teams are learning and moving forward.

*Figure 8.1: Characteristics of successful innovation cultures.*

On the other hand, Google has a "20%-time" policy, which encourages Google employees to spend 20% of their time working on what they think will most benefit the company. The idea is that it will inspire Google employees to be more creative and innovative. Many successful products from Google, such as Gmail and Adsense, originated from this policy. However, it is not clear if this policy still exists for all the projects at Google as for some of the projects, it is difficult to take time off from the day-to-day activities. In this case, it translates more to overtime than to "20%-time". In the end, the fact that employees are using their current project time or work overtime is not the most important. In both cases, it empowers employees to work on their ideas as long as they manage their day-to-day projects to the satisfaction of their managers.

Though corporations generally have an R&D department, innovation should not only be happening in R&D. It should be the job of everyone in the company, as long as they are willing and motivated to do so. As highlighted by the success of Amazon, it begins by being customer-centric and encouraging and promoting diversity of thoughts and background. Increasing the people in the company taking the innovation journey and finding these people in your company will enhance your chances to succeed. Celebrating small successes and the learning that occurs along the innovation path will go a long way toward creating an innovation culture, as hitting home runs often takes patience and perseverance.

To create a culture of innovation, leaders have an essential role to play. There is no better way to encourage innovation than to lead by example. Embracing change, being passionate and positive, and encouraging learning are some of the needed characteristics from an innovation leader. Innovation and change do not happen at once, so starting small, being resilient and flexible are keys to embracing corporate innovation. It is crucial to focus on employee engagement instead of focusing on ROI to create long-term sustainable change in your organization. Giving employees opportunities to focus on things that matter to them (e.g., via a policy like the Google "20%-time"), allows employees to be more creative and productive.

In the end, creating a culture of innovation is about focusing on the long term and sustainable change as opposed to focusing exclusively on short timeframes and ROI. It requires excellent support of the executive management and should be embedded in the company philosophy and vision to allow the company to continuously disrupt itself, before others do and reduce time to market.

## 8.2.  KILLING CORPORATE INNOVATION THEATER

A typical way for corporations to innovate is to create corporate innovation programs inside their R&D department and innovation outposts that are managed by their R&D department as, usually, R&D is synonymous with innovation. However, these innovation outposts rarely succeed when positioned in the corporate organization under managers who care more about their status and position than the long-term wellbeing of the company. Too many times, instead of doing the right thing for innovation, decisions are biased toward political convenience, toward the fear of making mistakes or toward merely doing what feels convenient. It is called *innovation theater,* as in this case, innovation teams do not focus on real innovation competency and making the world a better place. Innovation leaders who support innovation theater are "talking the talk" about corporate innovation and not "walking the walk" by removing barriers, ultimately preventing real innovation from happening. By paying lip service to change, they act against the building of an innovation culture which is critical for sustainable innovation.

As Steve Blank has pointed out in his blog post entitled "How to Avoid Innovation Theater" (Blank, 2015), when a corporation is faced with innovation theater, to move toward innovating the right way usually requires hands-on management from the CEO or the senior executive team. In case of the establishment of an innovation outpost, one of the first things that the executive management team needs to do is to be clear about the role that the innovation outpost will play. More specifically, how it fits into the corporate innovation portfolio, the amount of risk that they are willing to assume, the results expected, and the timeline associated with the business targets selected.

Corporate innovation programs are always looking for new ideas. The problem is that often new ideas are not going anywhere, because there is not an execution plan around the new ideas generated and corporate antibodies are quick to come up with reasons why the new proposals are not executable. It is essential to have a comprehensive approach about how to turn these ideas into minimum viable products, pilots, or proof-of-concepts to prevent this from happening. You should also ensure that you are sponsored from the top of the organization and that the innovation program links into the company strategy with a clear execution plan. The point highlighted here is that planning both the front-end and back-end of innovation together and connecting them before investing much money on the innovation front-end is essential. Understanding where to innovate according to your corporate strategy and how to execute and scale innovation will create the conditions for a successful innovation path. You also want to ensure that your approach remains flexible and can adapt over time as learning will dictate the exact route that you should follow. In the end, being able to win over innovation theater comes down to sound management practices, excellent communication between all the parties involved, top executive involvement, and excellent execution.

## 8.3. WHY LARGE COMPANIES STRUGGLE WITH INNOVATION AND THE CHALLENGES OF CONSTANT REINVENTION FACED BY CORPORATIONS

Xerox invented many of the technologies that we use in personal computing today but failed to capitalize on them. Kodak invented the digital camera but filed for bankruptcy in 2012. Sony had everything to be able to continue to be a leader in the digital music player space, but Apple disrupted the industry and came up with the iPod. Nokia was one of the leading players in the smartphone space and lost the battle to the iPhone. Why do large companies, who once were very successful, have trouble staying at the top of their industry? *Figure 8.2* shows some of the most common reasons, also detailed in the following paragraphs.

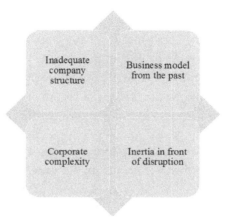

Inadequate company structure

Business model from the past

Corporate complexity

Inertia in front of disruption

*Figure 8.2: Most common corporate challenges.*

The truth is that corporations that have been successful often fail to innovate because they keep making the kind of choices that made them prosperous in an earlier environment. In short, knowledge and success can be the enemies of innovation. Even when the world changes around them, corporations tend to have a hard time adapting quickly enough to these changes. Corporations often struggle when innovation requires a new organizational structure (e.g., the proposed innovation does not fit into an existing business unit). An example is Xerox with the laser printer. One of the reasons often mentioned for Xerox's failure to capitalize on this innovation is that short-sighted managers managed the bottom line instead of thinking about the future. Frequently corporations are vertically integrated and are managed as silos which work separately. However, a new business may necessitate business units to work together. It is a structural change that corporations often fail to achieve.

Organizational changes are often hard to implement for organizations which exist based on a business model that has been successful in the past. The amount of the changes needed and the willingness of the company leadership to drive these changes will ultimately determine success. It is one of the significant challenges to drive progress on an ongoing basis. The corporate executive management needs to be actively involved to continuously adapt the company structure to support innovation and new business models. Dominant organizations often see the disruption coming and have a sound understanding of the future. However, due to corporate inertia, they often fail to put together the right response that will allow innovation to be successful. The job of modern corporate CEOs is to uncouple the life cycle of their company from the life cycle of their current business.

Dealing with corporate complexity is another reason why a corporation struggles with innovation. Politics, corporation inertia, the lack of mechanisms for Seed-level funding, the time that it takes to have business units buy into an idea and the inability for corporate antibodies to see the future bring a high level of complexity that is often killing innovation. Innovation needs a streamlined approach, and it requires a simple process and approval procedures along with the proper incentives and the identification of internal champions who will carry it through. When innovation is fitting in the existing company structure, it also necessitates close cooperation between the innovation team and the business unit. The importance of the transition between the innovation team and the business unit is, typically, underestimated. Creating accountability and incentives for success is essential together with close management from senior executives to make sure that the innovation team hits its milestones and that nothing is falling through the cracks.

To generate innovation, corporations used to focus internally via R&D departments. More recently, they adopted open innovation and built innovation outposts to scout technologies or leverage corporate venturing to invest in startups and build strategic collaborations. Today corporations tend to be focused geographically on specific innovation ecosystems (such as Plug and Play in Silicon Valley). It means that corporations need to increase engagement with the different stakeholders of the ecosystems such as entrepreneurs, other corporations, Universities, and VCs. However, by engaging with ecosystems, they need to be adopting a more experimental approach and be patient in receiving the fruits of their effort as it may take some time to get results. They also need to be mindful about how to integrate the results inside the organization, as they will have to get the corporate antibodies on board or out of the way.

Innovation is a process, and some companies, such as Amazon, are more consistently successful at delivering innovations and disrupting themselves. These organizations have some common characteristics that are summarized below:

- They have clear principles and vision about where they want to go and a sound strategy to get there.
- They are customer-centric, continuously gathering data that feeds their execution plan.
- They are market leaders and always hungry for the next innovation to make the world a better place. It is their way of staying on top.
- They strive to understand their customers and are continually looking for new customer insights to remain relevant and discover new business opportunities. They always experiment to find the right path.
- They are very disciplined and focused when making innovation decisions, and very good at executing. They rely on a well-defined execution process that can monetize the ideas coming from the innovation front-end.
- They have strong, focused, and principle-oriented innovation leaders that allow them to create an innovation culture across their business units, which is enabling them to stay consistently relevant and hungry for innovation.

The above allows corporations to keep up with the ever-increasing speed of change and to overcome the challenges of constant innovation by consistently delivering better value for their markets and penetrating new markets to fuel their growth.

## 8.4. FOCUSING ON THE SHORT TERM AND A QUICK ROI KILLS TRANSFORMATIVE INNOVATION

Why do new businesses fail in large organizations? Often, it is because they misalign the short and long term. By aligning the short-term objectives with the company's long-term goals, the organization can create incremental milestones, create small wins, and potentially adjust the strategy according to the evidence gathered to reach this long-term goal. One of the main reasons for corporations to emphasize the short term at the expense of targets further in the future is that they want to hit the numbers. When creating a new business—until finding a repeatable business model—a business plan is just a guess. However, corporations often create the new business in a way similar to the old one, for example by placing the new venture inside a sales division who will run the new business using the same KPIs as their current business. Doing so will usually result in killing the new venture. Sales organizations tend to focus on proven business instead of an uncertain and yet unproven business.

Investors and expectations for short-term financial gains create pressure for immediate results. It can lead to missing the long-term future, especially when the new business is not mature enough, and shortcuts are being taken to satisfy short-term requests. Short-term strategies should align with the organization's long-term goals. However, corporations hate uncertainty, and long-term objectives are, by definition, uncertain. They tend to overanalyze, and often consider new opportunities unworthy unless they will result in short-term gains. Transformative innovation takes time and asking teams to prove quickly that a prospective opportunity is viable is generally a big mistake. Long-term objectives that can help you transform your business or create a new business pillar need experimentation to de-risk them with the understanding that they may not work. This is what it takes to disrupt yourself instead of being disrupted. As shown in *Figure 8.3*, in the end, innovation should be looked at as a portfolio, including:

- Short-term opportunities. They tend to be extensions or enhanced features of current product lines.
- Medium-term business. They require more time and have a higher risk because the uncertainty increases.
- Long-term disruptions. They often identify a problem without a clear solution and will allow you to leapfrog your competition if you are the one providing the solution.

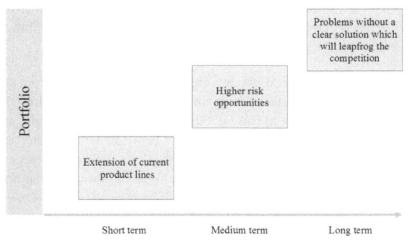

*Figure 8.3: Innovation should look at a portfolio of opportunities.*

Each company should identify the right mix according to the amount of risk that is acceptable. The long-term opportunities identified should align with the long-term company strategy and its vision of the future.

## 8.5. SCALING WITH ADJACENT MARKETS AND TRANSFORMING THE CORE

As discussed in the previous sections, corporations have been successful at optimizing and monetizing their existing business. However, they often have difficulties in transforming themselves and creating new business. One question that is worth asking is how they could leverage their existing business to create transformative changes and achieve significant returns, instead of trying to develop disruptive innovations disconnected from their main business. One strategy is to focus on adjacent opportunities and identify opportunities that can be transformative. However, as shown in *Figure 8.4*, it is essential to treat, at least in the early stages, adjacent businesses differently from the core business as otherwise the chances of failure increase.

When companies try to create a significant change, they often fail as there is typically more uncertainty in the new business than the corporation is willing to handle. Furthermore, creating a significant change necessitates many resources. To deal with these two challenges, corporations tend to come back to their core business. An alternative is to innovate not too far from the core, as it requires much less time and resources and is much better understood. One of the keys is to do it with a mindset which has a long-term orientation and emphasizes experimentation and learning that can be used to transform the core instead of focusing on short-term returns. It is also essential that the adjacent market considers the technology and market trends that the corporation is seeing. Adjacent markets are generally more easily accepted internally, even by the corporate antibodies as they are more familiar and quicker to develop. Adjacent markets can leverage the technology and know-how established for a completely different area.

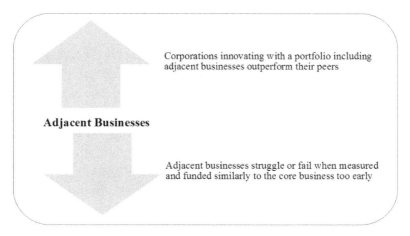

*Figure 8.4: Scaling with adjacent markets.*

Scaling with adjacent markets is an excellent way to grow if the corporation has the right skill set to go after them. The critical thing to pay attention to is that it is not about providing your products and services to new customers, but it is, instead, about providing your skills and capabilities to new markets. A hypothetical example could be a company like Adidas who, when going after a new sport like mountain climbing, would start by selling athletic footwear for that sport and then, after establishing itself, would expand into protective equipment and eventually into other accessories used in this sport.

Transforming the core business is a big challenge for many corporations. However, leveraging the current skill set and expertise with the vision and long-term commitment to changing the core business can be an excellent way to scale revenues in the short term. It can be done without any significant risky investment or time requirement while accumulating new knowledge and evidence that will allow the corporation to disrupt itself in the mid to long term. Transforming the core is not an easy task to undertake, and it requires a deep understanding of the market forces and technology changes. A more pragmatic and progressive approach, such as focusing on adjacent markets, tends to be better suited to the level of risk that many corporations are comfortable with by connecting short-term revenues to transformative growth.

## 8.6. REMOVING THE FEAR FROM FAILURE AND UNLEARNING

Typically, corporations do not like to talk about failures and are reluctant to discuss (at least externally) things that do not go according to plan. The metrics often used are ROI and product launches. Failure is often not acceptable, and there is a minimal emphasis placed on learning. The focus is mainly on the results obtained, and the journey does not matter much. Because of this, corporate employees have an intense fear of failure. However, failures bring out most of our learning and being able to capture this learning puts us in a better place to succeed in the future. By definition, innovation involves the exploration of new areas, so it is essential to build a culture that is tolerant of failures, though failures should not be due to incompetence. Incompetence itself should be looked after and suppressed.

Everybody is worried about failing, especially when we go out of our comfort zone. We need to reframe our goals to overcome the fear of failure. One way to do this is to expand our goal by redefining success and including learning, as there is always something to learn when things do not go as we expect. In Silicon Valley, failure is called experience. After a failure, it is also essential to go back and try to understand what went wrong, identify the positive aspects of the situation and the learning that occurred along with how to make the most out of it. Failure can teach us things about ourselves that we would never have learned otherwise. Some insights can come only through failure, and learning from these insights will help us tremendously in the future. Some strategies to remove the fear of failure include planning for the worst-case scenario and building contingency plans that can help you be more confident in moving forward. Viewing failure as a challenge also helps to create a challenge mindset and prepares you for handling the situation in front of you.

You need to overcome the fear of failure, but too much success may also be detrimental to future success, especially in light of the rapid changes that we are experiencing. As Barry O'Reilly reminds us in his book *Unlearn: Let Go of Past Success to Achieve Extraordinary Results*

(O'Reilly, 2019), corporations should not stand still, or else they risk becoming disrupted and sometimes obsolete. This is the fate of Nokia, Kodak, Sears, and others. How corporations achieve success in the past is unlikely to bring them success in the future as our world is continuously changing, and corporations need to rethink everything they are doing continually. If corporations stay in their comfort zone and do not embrace uncertainty, they will fail to get after the new trends and will be late to the game. Corporations need to let go of the past, cultivate a curious mind, think big, and learn fast via experimentation and a bias to action. Each piece of evidence and each morsel of learning feeds the next cycle of discovery, deemphasizing prior knowledge based on an enhanced awareness and the seeking of new avenues adapted to the current situations encountered. Speed is of the essence, and small steps and insights lead to big success. *Figure 8.5* emphasizes the negative consequences of fearing failures and the positive aspects of letting go of past achievements and unlearning.

Amazon has been a leader in unlearning and reinventing itself. By building a mindset and behaviors around learning and placing big bets, Amazon has become a leader progressively in several markets from e-commerce to computing infrastructure and smart home. Amazon also had many failures, such as the Fire Phone. However, Amazon used lessons learned from these failures positively to compete in the marketplace and reach new grounds by continuously projecting the company into the future, instead of fearing the future because things did not go as expected in the past. In the end, it is all about a mindset that triggers a set of behaviors which help to create success in the future.

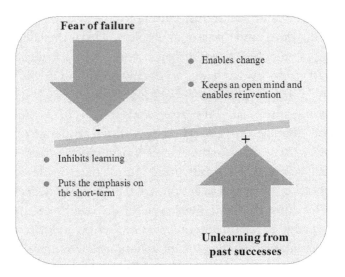

*Figure 8.5: The effects of the fear of failure and unlearning.*

## 8.7. HANDING OFF INNOVATION PROJECTS AND INTEGRATING THEM WITH THE CORE BUSINESS

If innovation projects are going to succeed, they'll need to survive a handoff from an innovation team to a business unit or an ad-hoc execution team. Every time that there is a project handoff, it increases the risk that a project may fall apart. Ad hoc innovation from R&D teams is not enough to be successful. It is necessary to align innovation initiatives with a plan to scale up promising ideas at the right time and when it makes sense. Innovation and the execution or "productization" of a new opportunity go hand in hand instead of being separate activities. One of the reasons that corporations have a hard time productizing some new ideas from R&D teams is that R&D is often an isolated department separated from the business units. Success necessitates a continuous feedback loop between the front-end and the back-end of innovation.

As shown in *Figure 8.6*, in a corporation, there are usually three units which are involved in the creation of new business opportunities:

- The R&D team, which is in charge of creating and exploring new ideas, generally a few years ahead. This team is comfortable with ambiguity and uses methods such as design thinking and lean startup.
- The advanced R&D, which is often vertically integrated with the business unit and in charge of the short-term opportunities, generally closely related to the business unit focus.
- The business unit, which is in charge of executing the current business, drives growth or improves operations.

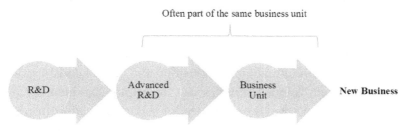

*Figure 8.6: The corporate units generally involved in new business creation.*

These units should be viewed as discrete parallel paths. The output of one unit does not necessarily flow into the next one, though the traditional way to hand off opportunities is to move them from the R&D team to the business unit via the advanced R&D group. However, it is essential to have early interactions and communications between those who are creating the business strategy and the associated goals and those who are delivering on these initial goals. These communications will allow the plan itself to evolve and improve. Unfortunately, today, the business strategy and execution are often viewed as separate steps from the innovation front-end, instead of being seen as a continuous learning cycle. It is a mistake and is a consequence of the silo model of corporate innovation. For innovation projects, such an organization increases the points of failure. This challenge needs to be better tackled by corporations who should focus on iterating the business goals and strategic plans while the front-end innovation team gathers insights. Handoffs should also be designed, tailored to the group receiving them and planned from the beginning.

Innovation has the highest chances to succeed by breaking down the organization's structural barriers so that new ideas can be diffused better across the organization. By removing these artificial separations and fostering a collaborative spirit, the innovation front-end team has a much easier time propagating new opportunities inside the corporation, and handing off projects is not as much of an issue anymore.

## 8.8. THE CHALLENGES OF OPEN INNOVATION FOR CORPORATIONS

To increase their chances of success, corporations are complementing their innovation toolbox using open innovation and tools such as corporate venturing, strategic partnerships, and startup collaborations. Via innovation outposts, they scout technologies, identify new opportunities and involve some parts of the organization in proof-of-concepts for validating the outpost's findings. The hope is that they can create speed by feeding the organization with new ideas and technologies.

One of the first challenges of open innovation is to build a culture of experimentation and to try new things even if the outcome is uncertain. Experimentation materializes in terms of proof-of-concepts to evaluate new technologies and identify the best solutions that can satisfy the corporation's needs. This is easy to say, as, for some corporations, it is a challenging task because they are not comfortable with experimentation. They look at open innovation more in terms of profit and loss instead of a way to learn, create future directions, and move forward ahead of their competition. Another challenge is to embed the open innovation inside the organization, instead of having a separate activity concentrating on open innovation. When it is an independent activity, the problem of handoff comes into play.

It is not uncommon that corporations are ill-prepared to execute open innovation because they do not have the expertise or the skills to run it. Open innovation requires an entrepreneurial mindset, to be open-minded, to be externally focused, to have excellent collaboration skills, and to build bridges between technology and business and internal and external stakeholders. It is all about creating win-win collaborations. While this is generally well understood, corporations do not always put people who have those skills and mindsets in charge of open innovation, decreasing their chances of success. Just as digital transformation requires a shift in mindset, so does open innovation. *Figure 8.7* summarizes the challenges described above.

*Figure 8.7: Corporate innovation challenges.*

## 8.9. ACCESSING EXTERNAL EXPERTISE AND INNOVATION ADVISORS/MENTORS

Just as corporations should use open innovation to create speed, corporations should access external expertise such as advisors and mentors, to complement their internal resources and draw on experience and skills in areas where they lack some. As technology development is progressing very rapidly, corporations have trouble adapting to the changes that are happening and fail to train their workforce to be competitive and stay relevant. Corporations are working with startups to solve their immediate needs, to create new areas, to compensate for their inability to adapt, and to accelerate innovation. Another way to acquire expertise and experience is to work with mentors, consultants, and advisors who can help corporations be more innovative in the following ways (also summarized in *Figure 8.8*):

- By being a source of ideas, as they often bring a new perspective not biased by corporate politics and context. This fresh look can complement internal activities and bring additional expertise, creativity, and inspiration. It can also facilitate new partnerships that would have been difficult to put in place by internal corporate members.
- By providing an external and unbiased validation and contributing to add further evidence that would strengthen the direction followed. Mentors/advisors are also better placed to give criticisms and feedback that can be very beneficial to the innovation team.
- By providing guidance about best practices from the external corporate world and providing access to their ecosystems such as accelerators, incubators, or specific experts.

*Figure 8.8: The different ways mentors/advisors can help.*

Today it is essential to realize that even the most powerful corporations cannot do things alone. By accessing external resources, such as mentors and advisors, corporations can add new perspectives to their innovation journey, challenge the innovation team, and by doing so, minimize their risk of failure. It is an excellent way to acquire temporary expertise and to adapt to the fast pace of change without requiring all the necessary resources to be available internally.

## 8.10. OVERCOMING THE CORPORATE ANTIBODIES AND THE IMPORTANCE OF SENIOR MANAGEMENT

Every corporation has some members who:

- Do not have incentives to innovate and only see the downside of taking risks.
- Think first about protecting their jobs and are more interested in doing what is politically right than what is suitable for the corporation.
- Are uncomfortable when thinking out-of-the-box and going out of their way to create new directions.
- Have a deep-rooted fear of a new business cannibalizing their current business.
- Have a strong desire to keep leveraging the status quo instead of creating new capabilities.

In this book, we call these corporate members antibodies as they feel threatened by disruptions, and more generally innovation that is going toward a direction different from what they are comfortable with, or activities that are going against their interest. Sometimes they want to be on the safe side. When corporate antibodies are managers or in a position to make decisions about innovation projects, they can be very detrimental to the innovation progress made by corporate innovation. Almost always, it is the behaviors triggered by the corporate environment which are threatening innovation, as the people themselves are generally not against blazing a new path to the future.

For antibodies, it often starts with the perception of failure, which is quite different in a startup as compared to a corporation. For a startup, it is a part of life, and failure brings learning and experience, while for a corporation which has its brand image on the line, failure is still difficult to accept. Startups tend to fail forward while, with corporations, failures tend to limit the level of risk they will take in the future. Different methods can be used to overcome the objections of corporate antibodies.

- If their ego gets in the way, it may be helpful to get their support by appealing to their ego and satisfying their need for personal validation. It can help in bringing innovation forward. Often there is no benefit to challenging them.
- If their objections arise because they do not believe that the corporation will be able to execute your new ideas due to past experiences, it may be helpful to understand their previous experiences and to show them how your new ideas are different.
- If they want to stay on the safe side, you can try to demonstrate that there is less risk than they might think and devise a stepwise approach where the first step will be low risk and will not necessitate a large amount of funding.

Corporate antibodies may believe deep inside that they are doing the right thing. The challenge is to convince them that your new ideas are worth trying and that your thoughts align with their values.

Another way to deal with the corporate antibodies is to bypass them and get direct support from senior management. It is often the fastest way to innovate given the need for quick decision-making and unconventional approaches, which usually do not fit with the traditional way of doing things by the current business. Today many executives understand that an essential part of their job is to be involved actively in their company innovation to remain competitive. However, there is a tension between the pressure to boost short-term results—such as next quarter's earnings—and the pressure to manage other long-term priorities which do not have a direct impact on the near-term bottom line.

Top management must have an active role in the company innovation to make sure that there is a strong alignment between the business strategy and the innovation strategy. It will help them support the creation of an innovation culture, motivate employees to innovate and have a good understanding of the context before making some decisions about which ideas to pursue. Often the role of senior management is only to point the way forward, show ownership, and make some of the important decisions after consulting their subordinates.

## 8.11. ALIGNING INNOVATION WITH THE CORPORATE STRATEGY

Creating new business opportunities in a corporation is a journey that involves many parts of the company from the creation of the initial idea and prototypes by the innovation team to product development to sales and marketing. Creating an internal alignment and an internal process around the objectives of the company allows each part of the organization to adapt its capabilities and apply the strategic goals to their activities so that innovative ideas transform into successful products and services. This is easier said than done. Many corporations understand this need but struggle to put in place an effective process. A few reasons include:

- Corporate leaders having low confidence in their innovation team to initiate the creation of new business opportunities. This is often due to past projects that have not been successful or some previous investments that did not yield satisfactory results.
- The increased popularity of open innovation and models which promote innovation both internally and externally to increase speed and search for talents and expertise outside the corporation. Open innovation is often embraced ahead of

R&D and innovation teams, making it challenging to create ahead of time an internal corporate strategy that propagates to the different relevant parts of the company.

- The growing importance of customers as a part of the innovation process to guide and validate innovation as companies are looking into products and services that do not exist and meet needs that customers do not yet know that they have. Due to the accelerating time to market and reliance on external resources, aligning the organization around innovation goals can sometimes be very challenging.

Innovation is about people coming together and collaborating inside and outside the organization for the creation of transformative solutions that create value and can be monetized. Because of the need for speed and collaboration to be competitive, the building of an innovation mindset and culture continuously woven into the everyday fiber of the business is progressively replacing strategic planning. Starting from the top, instead of innovation being crafted carefully by internal planning groups, cultivating an innovation mindset throughout the company provides a better understanding of customer needs and external innovation forces.

## 8.12. THE CORPORATE REQUIREMENTS FOR A DUAL APPROACH AND AN AMBIDEXTROUS ORGANIZATION

A corporation has to manage for today, taking care of the current business, and explore what is next to prepare for its future. This is very challenging to achieve because what is needed from the organization to succeed in the future as compared to today's business is quite different in terms of the approaches taken, the talents required, the mindset, and the way to measure success. This is known as ambidexterity (O'Reilly III & Tushman, 2004), and it is rare to find leaders who can manage both at the same time. Innovation requires a growth mindset where it is essential to be comfortable with ambiguity, strong convictions, and often chaos, while managing the current business is about execution, discipline, and process. Only a few organizations have excelled at both and could reinvent themselves while growing their current revenues. Often organizations need an existential crisis that triggers survival behaviors to reinvent themselves. *Figure 8.9* shows the essential characteristics of an ambidextrous organization that excels at both exploration and execution.

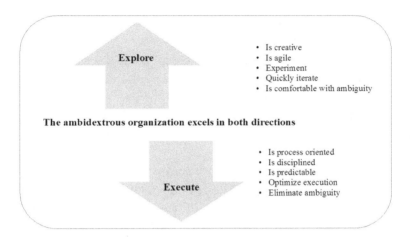

*Figure 8.9: Characteristics of an ambidextrous organization.*

The act of balancing exploration and execution is one of the toughest of all managerial challenges. Innovators are always curious, have a bias for action, love to explore, and understand that there is no innovation without experimentation. Execution does not leave room for experimental testing, as everything is expected to be well planned with clear metrics for success. Enabling an ambidextrous corporation is to find the balance between agility and execution. An ambidextrous corporation competes in new markets and technologies that enable the firm to survive in the face of changing market conditions. Within the organization, exploration and execution compete for scarce resources, and managers often tend toward less risky, short-term incremental innovation. It is essential to shield the innovation branch of the organization from the demand of the execution branch and to apply a different set of KPIs to solve the tensions between the two. When KPIs emphasize short-term output, efficiency, and near-term gains, innovation is likely to fail.

The main characteristics of an ambidextrous organization are as follows:

- A strategic vision that ties together exploration and execution.
- Leaders that own both exploration and execution strategies and communicate them inside the organization.
- Separate but aligned structures, one for experimentation and one for carrying out the current business that leverages the organization's core assets.
- The ability of the top management to deal with the tensions between exploration and execution when they arise.

On the other hand, organizations which struggle with ambidexterity tend to fall into the following habits:

- The current business model dominates the agenda.
- Directions follow internal guesses and untested business plans.
- Top management focuses mainly on execution and is too busy to handle innovation.
- The company is obsessed with competitors more than customers.
- Focus on technology instead of the market.
- Organize innovation and execution as separate silos.
- Integrate new opportunities too quickly in the execution engine.

One element that is very important for an ambidextrous organization is the allocation of funding between exploration and execution. In many organizations, innovation funding is highly variable from year to year, making the creation of new business opportunities very challenging. Innovation needs protected funding to avoid continuous shifts of directions and resources. Organizational ambidexterity is a vital requirement for modern corporations. It requires top management and leaders who have the ability, willingness, and mindset to juggle skillfully between exploration and execution. It is not an easy task, and this kind of leadership is rare. As always, it is about how organizational ambidexterity is implemented and executed, more than the strategy itself, that is key to a successful journey.

## 8.13. MEASURING SUCCESS

How to measure innovation and success, and what are the right KPIs to use has been well documented. However, in contrast with current business measured with objective KPIs such as revenue growth and the number of acquired customers, innovation tends to be more abstract and concrete metrics like financial metrics can be challenging to define. Instead of accounting metrics, soft metrics like overall customer interest, the number of ideas generated, or employee engagement are sometimes used by companies to track their innovation progress. These metrics are useful as they often measure your company innovation culture and mindset toward innovation. Innovation comes from motivated employees and understanding how your company approaches innovation is critical to long-term success. Of course, these soft metrics often need to be combined with more tangible ones such as the number of prototypes created, the number of patents filed or the number of transfers to business units. Specific metrics depend on what the innovation team wants to achieve, and tailoring them to innovation objectives is essential. So, it is best to establish your goals and then to define the metrics that will allow you to track your progress toward the goals you set. As your goals change, you need to adapt the way you measure your progression.

Corporations need to measure their innovation and core business activities differently. In both cases, it is crucial to define KPIs to track progress and change course if required, but as mentioned, you need to use different KPIs. In the case of innovation, these KPIs also need to be adapted as innovation moves through different innovation stages. In the early stages, up to the product-market fit, the following indicators can be used:

- Validation velocity indicating how fast you are making progress and your rate of learning. This indicator can, for example, track how many hypotheses were tested. Learning should be followed by quick actions, as actions will enable progress.

- Cost per failure showing how well you are doing in managing your failed initiatives. To be successful and to maximize the use of limited resources, it is essential to be able to prune the dead branches early in the process. The lesson here is to prototype and test early and frequently.

These two metrics make sense, especially in the early stages. *Figure 8.10* shows how these metrics evolve during the innovation stages. The validation velocity metric allows a company to minimize risks, especially when the new venture is pre-revenue. It is crucial to be able to measure how close to a significant business the new venture is and to quickly gather evidence that will reduce the risks that the new venture will build something that the market does not want. When innovating, picking a winner is the challenge. So, the idea is to initially invest a small amount of funding in each innovation project and to set up metrics, such as the validation velocity, that will help reduce the risks and pick the top ones. Metrics guide behaviors and understanding the innovation metrics to use for reducing the risks is essential. Innovation teams need to make the difference between activities and risk reduction. Carefully selected measures of progress help teams focus on risk reduction by concentrating on validating quickly the relevant hypotheses that are necessary for the project to have a chance to be successful. Innovation teams know that they collected sufficient evidence by analyzing customer feedback and engagement.

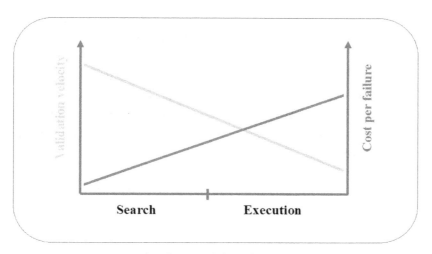

*Figure 8.10: Evolution of the validation velocity and
cost per failure during the innovation stages.*

As innovation is progressing through the innovation roadmap, other
types of indicators are used, such as:

- The number of problem–solution fits, supported by evidence
  that you have found a solution for this market need.
- The number of product–market fits, supported by evidence
  that the market is happy with the product/service developed.

By definition, we cannot separate innovation and failures. However,
by looking at new business creation through an innovation portfolio
and continuously looking at portfolio metrics, it is easier to convince
the top company leadership to invest. Inevitably, many innovation
projects will not survive. However, the ones succeeding will justify
the investment. The project-level metrics will allow the top projects
to rise to the top, while the portfolio-level metrics help explain the
innovation investment.

Finally, as innovation moves internally toward a product launch and execution by the business units, the following KPIs are often used:

- The number of transfers to the business units so that business units can productize and launch the new business.
- The contribution to revenues from the innovation group (though it is sometimes difficult to measure as it is not always a direct contribution).

While the KPIs above are not the only ones to use, they indicate some of the metrics that can be put in place to continuously track the progress made and the contribution of innovation to the long-term success of the company.

## 8.14. THE INNOVATION CHALLENGES OF ASIAN ORGANIZATIONS

In this section, I will share my direct experience obtained during my tenure at Panasonic for over 25 years. Asian countries differ in many respects, but also have many similarities. The following paragraphs will emphasize some general characteristics that are present in a country like Japan, but also to some extent in other Asian countries, and show how they impact innovation as compared to the Western world. In many countries, cultural context is essential, and it is beneficial to understand how this cultural context affects innovation. The points below explain in part some of the innovation challenges faced by Japan and to some degree by other Asian countries, though, as mentioned, differences exist.

- There is a strong bias to act on behalf of the collective versus themselves as individuals. There is a group spirit leading to seeking collective agreements, harmony, and optimization of the status quo. It means that decisions tend to be slower as looking for consensus takes time. However, it also means that blame for failure cannot be pinned on one person in the organization; this blaming is seen as puerile: if the group is failing, all members must pitch in and help. It is very different from the individualism of Western cultures.

- There is an established hierarchy and accurate control of the uncertainty, which leads to risk avoidance. Everybody has a role and accepts the hierarchical order. It is a challenge for innovation as this mindset, in practice, makes employees defer to the next level above instead of creatively arguing for outcomes. This cultural standpoint limits innovation. Cultural attitudes are powerful. If people hesitate to share their ideas, their thoughts, their feelings, and their frustrations, then innovation gets marginalized.

- It is important to create a safe psychological environment so that people feel taken care of by the organization. At all levels, safety and security are first. Failure is not an option, as failure has much stronger negativity associated with it than in the United States.

- Some Asian countries, such as Japan have a "monochronic" culture where individuals generally do one thing at a time. It can be an advantage as it can provide a strong focus, attention to details, punctuality and promptness in meeting deadlines but it can also be a disadvantage as the lack of structure and chaos often brought by innovation are sometimes challenging to handle.

- Asian countries like China and Japan are home to *top-class manufacturing*. In the case of Japan, this is rooted in the rich craftsmanship tradition, "monodzukuri," as evidenced by the degree of perfection in Samurai swords. On the other hand, anything that is not tangible can be more difficult. It explains to some degree why Japan has been struggling with software. On the other hand, China has been making substantial progress in new technologies such as Artificial Intelligence (AI), so, at least in China, a change is happening.

All the points above constitute challenges that can impact innovation. Of course, Asian cultures also have many characteristics which are helping the creation of change, such as the notion of continuous improvement and a strong capability of adaptation. However, the purpose of this section was mainly to focus on some of the innovation challenges that Asian organizations face.

## 8.15. FROM CORPORATE R&D TO INNOVATION LABS AND STARTUP ENGAGEMENT

The rate at which technology is disrupting companies is accelerating. Corporations have to adapt their structures and activities to keep pace with the changes that are happening. During the 20th century, the typical corporate approach to innovation was to establish a corporate R&D department which was internally focused, well-funded, and was developing technology secretly. The focus was on creating intellectual property, enhancing external visibility about the company innovation effort, publishing papers at conferences and from time to time transferring technologies to business units. The research conducted at companies such as Xerox PARC in Silicon Valley, Bell Laboratories, and Japanese corporations like NTT, Panasonic, and Sony illustrated this approach. In the 90s, it became clear that corporate R&D could not keep up with the accelerating pace of advances in technologies (e.g., information technology). Technology innovation could not create the expected growth in revenues, and it was necessary to develop other approaches such as the creation of innovation labs.

At the end of the 90s and for roughly the first ten years of the 21st century, innovation labs became a popular way for corporations to enhance and accelerate their innovation effort. They progressively adopted approaches such as design thinking and lean startup, and shifted the focus gradually from technology development to the creation of new business using business model innovation. It gave rise to corporate venture groups investing minority stakes into startups to create strategic partnerships. Open innovation became a way to bridge the gaps between current and future business. Innovation labs, often integrated into innovation hubs like Silicon Valley, became in charge of creating new ideas and methodologies often similar to the ones used in the world of entrepreneurship in hopes of developing the next big thing for the corporation. Innovation labs started to act like startups and incubate new projects using rapid prototyping and minimal viable products, while top management was encouraging employees to think like founders. Though the methodologies and goals are similar, there are significant differences between a startup and an innovation lab:

- A startup is not truly a startup without risk, and corporations do whatever they can to minimize risk.
- Innovation labs are often late to the game as by the time the corporation decides on an innovation direction and funds it, somebody else is already working on it, and the corporation will play catch-up.
- As innovation labs are working on many different types of ideas, they approach a new business opportunity often as a generalist in contrast with a startup where founders eat and breathe the area they are developing.
- Because startups do not have to deal with corporate politics, hierarchies, and corporate decision processes, they can act much quicker than innovation labs.
- Startups focus on one project and dedicate all their resources to this project being successful, while innovation labs tend to aim at multiple targets.

These differences explain why it is difficult for innovation labs to act like startups. They also do not have the incentives that startups have if successful. It led to the birth of innovation outposts which often are set up at the center of an innovation ecosystem, such as Silicon Valley, where they can connect to many startups. These innovation outposts, instead of trying to create the next big thing, scout technologies from startups, serve as a technology window, gather business and technology intelligence about emerging trends, and connect startups to the business units. Their goal is to create pilot programs which will help to validate the startup technology using the corporation's channel and resources. Plug and Play at the heart of Silicon Valley in Sunnyvale, California, is a startup ecosystem which facilitates the matchup between corporations and startups.

Corporation-startup engagement is the current trend as it allows the corporation to adapt to the hectic pace of innovation by leveraging its channels, brand, and resources and combining them with startup technology to create new capabilities. Corporation-startup engagement relies on the establishment of trusted and respected relationships between corporations and startups, instead of substantial internal corporate developments. Of course, the challenge is the speed at which corporations can engage with startups and the level of risk that they can accept to deal with the uncertain outcome before they immerse into pilots. More information about how corporations can collaborate with startups is available in the next chapter.

## 8.16. THE CHALLENGES OF EXPERIMENTING IN A LARGE CORPORATION

Large corporations have a history and a reputation or brand to protect. Due to their structure, the primary contacts with customers come from the sales force. At the same time, innovation involves a deep customer understanding and much experimentation. It creates a tension between protecting the brand and innovating. Another challenge is that corporations need to experiment while being in full compliance with the law. Startups often navigate the gray areas of the law. How well a corporation can address these tensions often determines its ability to succeed.

There are several ways to deal with those tensions, especially in the initial innovation stages:

- Selecting a group of customers who know that they are providing a service in exchange for a reward.
- Communicating to customers that they will help the creation of future products.

- Targeting early adopters who are often curious to get ahold of new products.
- Forging a good partnership with the corporate lawyers, so that they become active allies instead of bringing up unnecessary barriers that stifle creativity.

In the initial innovation stages, it is often possible to find a workaround and create a collaboration between the sales and the innovation teams to access targeted customers. The problem is more challenging to deal with at the later stages when the product is ready to be launched, and validation will come from the customers buying the product or not. It is the ultimate validation, as until customers are willing to pay for the product, there is no certainty that the product will be successful in the marketplace. It is not unusual for customers to provide some feedback in the early stages and act in a different way when they need to spend their money to buy the product.

To deal with the experimentation challenges, P&G created a specialized organization called LearningWorks, whose role was to provide a business process for smaller-scale business, an innovation engine able to quickly execute and customize cost-effective initiatives, and a flexible supply chain ready to bring products to market (Brown & Anthony, 2011). It is an example of what corporations can do to experiment without incurring the risk of damaging their brand.

# CHAPTER 9

## The Future of Corporate Innovation

### 9.1. THE NEW WAY OF MANAGING INNOVATION BY LEVERAGING STARTUP ECOSYSTEMS

For corporations, innovating used to be trendy and a useful marketing tool. However, today, it is a matter of life and death. Engaging with startups is now a vital part of corporate innovation and digital transformation. Many corporations have reduced their R&D effort as they have been struggling to adapt to the pace of change and, in many ways, have started to outsource R&D to the startup and venture community. As a result, corporations are hoping to speed up innovation and gain first-mover advantage in their markets. Collaborations between startups and corporations, if done right, can benefit both sides as it helps corporations enter new markets and startups validate their products and scale. As shown in *Figure 9.1,* a corporation can "pull" startups toward the corporation by identifying those most relevant to its business or vision using various methods such as partnership, investment, or acquisition to benefit the corporation. Another way is to "push" some internal innovations toward the startup ecosystem to help them develop, to minimize risks by bringing external resources, or to free them from the corporate structure. This section will mainly cover the "pull" aspect of how corporations can leverage startup ecosystems.

The success of a startup-corporation collaboration has a lot to do with expectations, culture, the work ethic of both parties, and clearly defined roles and responsibilities. It is essential for corporations to provide startups with value and to invest in the relationships with entrepreneurs, as this is what it takes to build an excellent reputation. By establishing a clear corporate window with the startups, corporations can also facilitate and guide the relationships, which is essential to avoid miscommunication and confusion. Finally, speed is critical. A lengthy process of negotiation aiming at decreasing risk can be very detrimental to the relationship and the success of the collaboration. Successful collaborations are generally quick and flexible, and the corporations who can best leverage relationships with startups often understand that all the nuts and bolts of the partnership are not entirely clear in the initial phase of the collaboration.

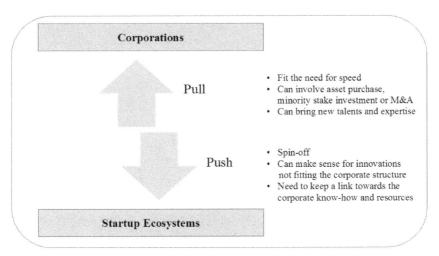

*Figure 9.1: Innovating by leveraging startup ecosystems.*

To engage with startups, more and more corporations are partnering with dedicated ecosystems such as, in the San Francisco Bay Area, 500 Startups or Plug and Play. These ecosystems help corporations source startups and facilitate pilot programs. Plug and Play, for example, matches up large corporations with startups in an innovation ecosystem that results in partnership opportunities, joint ventures, investments, and acquisitions all focused on creating the next big thing. Corporations can have access to many industry verticals (about 15 at the time of this writing, such as healthcare and mobility) to understand trends, technologies, and startup companies leading the field for each vertical. A startup ecosystem, such as Plug and Play, provides a way to decrease the risk for the various ecosystem stakeholders. The corporations which are participating in the ecosystem vet the accelerated startups, increasing the probability for pilots. VCs also benefit, as they often co-invest in startups that already have collaborations in place with large corporations that can provide resources and channels, allowing the startups to scale quickly.

In this startup-corporation model, the trend is toward early-stage interactions. A growing number of corporations are looking at flexible partnerships with early-stage companies where both sides take a risk and can share the rewards. It is a change for corporations that, in the past, have been mainly acquiring startups or engaging in partnerships when the startups were more mature with proven technology. For startups, working with corporations is often the fastest route to market as corporations can allow them to optimize their products and globalize their product quickly with channels and processes already in place. Startups tend to innovate closer to customer needs, as they are not bound to corporate standards and procedures, and they can adapt and customize quickly based on customer feedback. This is beneficial to corporations, as it provides them with more freedom to develop disruptive solutions. In contrast to past practices where the relationships between startups and corporations were more biased toward acquisitions and less balanced, today both parties tend to look for win-win relationships, and corporations often meet startups on "equal footing."

Collaboration between corporations and startups is always a challenge to the mindsets on both sides, as the creative behaviors of entrepreneurs always challenge standardized corporation processes. Corporations often feel that startups have the wrong expectations, and entrepreneurs may think that corporations do not take them seriously, do not have a similar sense of urgency, or do not sufficiently value the collaboration. Aligning expectations at the beginning of the engagement is essential for enabling a successful partnership.

## 9.2. CO-CREATION AND COLLABORATIVE INNOVATION

Companies engage in co-creation projects to create customer value and a competitive advantage. Co-creation can take place with suppliers, distributors, or customers, and it is quickly replacing the traditional approach, which views innovation as a purely internal activity. However, there is generally not much guidance about how to execute it besides customer-driven approaches, such as design thinking and lean startup. The core idea behind co-creation is to engage people to create valuable experiences while enhancing network economics. Co-creation can be organized, managed, and facilitated. An example of a co-creation process is IBM's InnovationJam™. Pioneered by IBM in 2001, it consists of large-scale Internet-enabled brainstorming events where participants work together to identify new opportunities and come up with potential solutions.

A particular case of collaborative innovation is an innovation-focused alliance between companies to create value and drive business growth (Miles, 2005). Apple has been very successful with this collaborative innovation model by partnering with hundreds of companies for the development and growth of the iPhone. By driving growth and creating value, collaborative innovation benefits both the partnering companies and consumers. However, even though collaborative innovation may sound easy, many companies struggle with it. To be successful, it requires a non–adversarial mindset, a company structure adapted to collaborations, and the seeking of win–win collaboration outcomes. With the ever-accelerating time to market, companies cannot do everything alone, and collaborative innovation allows them to act faster and be smarter so that they can create economic growth. This realization is giving rise to new collaborative innovation approaches. *Figure 9.2* shows several external actors typically involved in collaborative innovation with corporations.

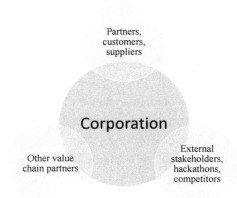

Partners, customers, suppliers

**Corporation**

Other value chain partners

External stakeholders, hackathons, competitors

*Figure 9.2: Creating value via co-creation and collaborative innovation with external actors.*

When collaborative innovation involves competitors, it is often called coopetition. Some examples include two competitors joining forces to enter a new market or to create economies of scale, the creation of a joint venture for a complementary business, or intellectual property cross-licensing. Coopetition focuses on a win–win relationship, rather than a win–lose deal. In this case, both partners should not forget that they are competitors and an agreement outlining what is off-limits is necessary to manage expectations and the collaboration areas. Coopetition involves weighing the risks against the benefits carefully before entering into a collaborative agreement.

Collaborative innovation can result in differentiation and can be a solution to quickly access fast-expanding markets. Today, even huge businesses risk rapidly becoming irrelevant, as the technological changes and the speed of communication have altered the rate at which markets evolve. Companies can capitalize on collaborative innovation in creative ways to deal with unanticipated market conditions.

## 9.3. DEVELOPING A SENSE OF PURPOSE WITHIN LARGE CORPORATIONS

Corporations are facing heightened competition and need to differentiate themselves. While technology breakthroughs used to be a means to do this, in the modern world, customer engagement, business innovation, and brand innovation are taking center stage. Many customers are attracted to brands that can make an overall positive impact on the future and will enable them and others to live in a better world. As a result, corporations are paying more attention to mission-driven products and taking actions toward creating a measurable social impact.

To build social impact and improve their bottom lines, corporations need to weave purpose into their product development and take actions that can impact society as a whole. For example, Panasonic, known for its slogan "A Better Life, A Better World," emphasizes sustainability and environment issues by developing technologies aimed at improving energy-saving and manufacturing processes to reduce the amount of energy consumption. Apple is also very focused on the environment by running the company on 100% renewable energy while trying to bring education to the mainstream and being a strong advocate for people's privacy due to the potential risks brought by new technologies. Google, via Google.org, is supporting global challenges focusing on ways to use AI to address societal challenges. These examples illustrate a trend toward social responsibility and helping others live a better life. By committing to a higher purpose, companies can increase partnership opportunities with other companies that have a similar goal. It also creates new insights by solving problems that many people care about and thereby pushes the boundaries of what is possible, building a better world.

Providing meaning is essential to attract and motivate employees. As shown in *Figure 9.3*, purpose lies at the intersection of solving problems that matter, connecting with the company customer core values, and business objectives that ensure there is a business to create. In areas with intense competition, such as Silicon Valley, it is becoming harder to attract employees with traditional methods such as wages and perks. Increasingly, people choose to spend their lives on things that matter. As a result, people are willing to trade a portion of wealth that could be available to them in order to achieve meaning and purpose. The natural and economic context, such as global warming or the growing gap between rich and poor, emphasizes this shift. People want to be part of a world that can enable finding solutions to these problems. The concept that a "sense of purpose" is going in the opposite direction of profitability is outdated. Today, it is no longer the case. It is quickly becoming a competitive advantage. Successful companies use purpose to drive their entire business strategy from the way the company organizes itself, to whom it hires and how the company develops.

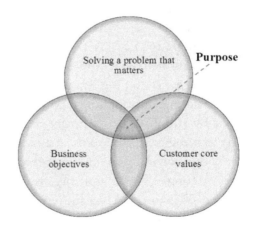

*Figure 9.3: Important elements involved in the development of a company purpose.*

Being a purpose-focused company is not an easy task. It is a process which necessitates continuous improvements. It will allow the company to retain its employees longer and will enable them to work better as the company and the employees are working toward the same goals. Customers will be more engaged, and in many cases will want to be a part of the company mission and contribute to the difference that it can make in the world. It becomes a win–win for everyone involved, and it helps drive talent, business success, and customer satisfaction.

## 9.4. CORPORATIONS SHOULD DEVELOP A CULTURE OF LIFELONG LEARNING AND UNLEARNING

Today the availability of technology building blocks and automation using Artificial Intelligence (AI) is replacing many tasks. The work of many employees is evolving progressively as smarter and smarter software and physical (e.g., robotics) tools are handling jobs usually done by people. It is changing the way employees need to develop and look at their jobs. More and more, employees need to adapt quickly and use cognitive skills to maximize the impact that they can have inside an organization. It is something that company leaders should consider carefully. In today's fast-paced environment, it is not possible to hire skills on demand, as a reactive approach is not quick enough to take advantage of new opportunities. It is essential to be proactive and continuously improve employees' skills. Lifelong learning is becoming central to the employees' job.

It used to be, and to some extent still is in many companies, that employees were periodically brushing up their skills by learning some new technologies, such as programming languages or tools. While this is still useful for some of the employees, it is increasingly essential for people to learn "soft" skills such as empathy, collaborative behaviors, and how to make decisions as employees will need to use complex cognitive skills more and more. *Figure 9.4* shows some of the soft skills that can allow employees to adapt to different types of job. For companies, this is becoming a competitive advantage. It is not enough anymore to own the tools and the technology if the knowledge of how to best take advantage of them and make complex decisions about how to leverage them inside and outside the company is not present. Those skills come with practice and experimentation. You do not learn them in the classroom. Companies need to create an environment where employees can learn and develop these skills so that they are available when the company needs them. Corporations that embrace experimentation are comfortable with uncertainty and ambiguity. They experiment to learn rather than focus on developing a product they will launch immediately.

*Figure 9.4: Soft skills that it is essential to learn.*

Paradoxically, as learning is happening in every aspect of the organization, companies need to continuously reinvent themselves and also unlearn much of what made their success in the past. Companies can become victims of their success. When successful, corporations tend to maintain the status quo and often lack a sense of urgency to continuously disrupt themselves. It is especially true when they have the means available and are doing well that they should seek new avenues for growth. A company like Amazon has been very successful at doing this, for example, by developing the AWS infrastructure business while being very successful in the e-commerce area. Corporations need to continuously look for new perspectives, be curious, and always look for a world that could be different from their current one. They also need to always be hungry for new business, think big, and experiment. Before corporations get disrupted by the competition, they need to figure out how to disrupt their business to create the next one. It necessitates effective leaders who understand that their organization needs to continually adapt to the pace of change even when they are successful, as previous success and behaviors may limit their potential and performance in the future.

Unlearning is hard, much harder than learning, as it is counter-intuitive to let go what has been successful. It takes a leader with an open mind who is not afraid to try, not afraid to possibly fail, and always facing toward the future. It also necessitates the willingness to explore and accept findings and insights that may be initially counter-intuitive with a strong desire to question them and to engage in figuring out if they could lead to some new opportunities. For example, streamed media is progressively replacing stored media, due to the availability of network bandwidth and streaming technologies which enabled this new reality and created a new consumer demand. As companies are looking into reinventing themselves, they need to focus on developing their employees or hiring new talent that is curious, willing to learn, dares to push for change, and can question the status quo.

## 9.5. FOCUSING ON PEOPLE, NOT ONLY NEW IDEAS AND TECHNOLOGY

As mentioned in the previous section, developing employees is essential to being able to compete. During the continuous transformation of the company, there is no more critical process than getting the right talent to the right role and continually developing employees' skills. Innovation is much more than just a technology invention or a new product/service development. It is about connecting personal beliefs and passion with customer needs and business goals. Embedding it in every aspect of an organization is imperative.

Today speed is essential, and innovation is happening at a pace never seen before. Corporations often fail to innovate as they are emphasizing the result of innovation programs, instead of investing in the innovators and the mindset or the culture, which are the enablers that connect the dots between customer needs, passion, purpose, and business. It is nearly impossible to dictate a mindset or an innovation culture. It is something that propagates from the top by demonstrating consistently in the company that innovation is a real priority, that it is valued and is part of the company culture. It is every employee's responsibility to do this, starting from the top.

When people think about innovation, they often think of good ideas. However, ideation is only a small part of the innovation process. There are more good ideas than there is the capacity to execute. One of the significant differences between innovative companies and the others is execution and the strategic use of new ideas within the company. Most of the time, companies have more ideas than they can use. They are just not making good use of them. Today, corporations who are struggling to innovate do not have an idea or a technology problem. They often have a recognition problem. Many companies developing music players had the technologies and the ideas in front of them to develop the iPod, but none of them could recognize the opportunity, and Apple took advantage of it. To "recognize" an idea as an opportunity, it is necessary to connect things not connected in the past.

As mentioned in a previous section, employees need meaning and purpose. It is critical for the leadership team to instill the "why" behind what the company is doing and to cultivate a culture where all aspects of the organization support the answer to the "why." Creating core values and strong principles, and maintaining those requires effort, but it connects employees to a higher mission, empowering them to achieve their goals. It is also essential for the leadership team to get to know employees' needs, capabilities, and desires, and to enable people to develop their skills and careers.

To create an innovation mindset and culture inside the company and to continuously develop employees' skills and decision-making, it is crucial to connect the employees with the company's mission. There is a need to emphasize that innovation is not only the objective of the innovation group, but it is everyone's job in the company. It is also important to embrace diversity, which is a necessary ingredient to be innovative and to develop a culture of experimentation while providing a fail-safe environment. As Amazon CEO Jeff Bezos mentioned, "Failure and invention are inseparable twins."

## 9.6.   INNOVATION MODELS FOR THE MODERN CORPORATION

Corporations are always looking to innovate faster and more successfully while using few resources. To do this, they are using different types of innovation models. *Figure 9.5* illustrates some of them. Each corporation has to figure out the best innovation model depending on their innovation objectives, resources available, and time-to-market should the innovation succeed. It is different for every corporation as it depends on what the company wants to achieve in the future.

On one end of the spectrum, there are closed innovation models illustrated by the traditional corporate R&D groups staffed by many scientists and technology specialists. The work happens mainly internally, and it generally requires a great deal of capital and time. It was popular a few decades ago, and while corporations still have corporate R&D departments, they are getting smaller and smaller. The modern corporation favors more open innovation models taking advantage of external collaborations to create speed, to access a large variety of resources, and to complement the knowledge and expertise available inside the corporation.

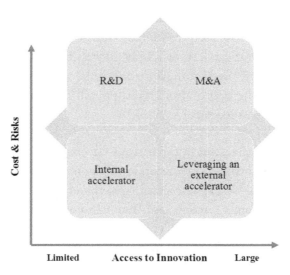

*Figure 9.5: Corporate innovation models.*

A corporate accelerator program is an example of a semi-open innovation model run internally, which leverages external resources via the startups participating in the accelerator. While such a program can benefit corporations, this model has some downsides for the startups, as it limits the partnerships that they can create while in the accelerator program. Startups can develop strong ties to one corporation, but they do not have any guarantee that the corporation will go forward with their technology.

Modern corporations tend to favor open collaboration models that they implement via innovation labs, innovation outposts, or by leveraging external accelerator ecosystems. Innovation labs have their dedicated innovation teams to create proof-of-concepts by leveraging external resources, design firms, or startups. Using rapid prototyping and sourcing technologies they develop prototypes and early-stage business opportunities that they can present to their business units which are in charge of executing them if they like the prototypes or if the business opportunities look promising. Innovation outposts, usually comprised of very few people, tend to have a liaison function between the ecosystem they belong to and the mothership. They identify technologies, startups, or business opportunities, report them to the mothership, which decides what to do with them. In the United States, Silicon Valley, Atlanta, and Boston are some popular locations for innovation outposts. To be successful, innovation labs and innovation outposts need to have strong links with other innovation programs inside the corporation. An innovation lab or an innovation outpost cannot be successful by itself.

Recently, one of the most popular ways for corporations to innovate is to leverage external accelerators and open innovation platforms that already exist. With these platforms, the corporation can decide on their level of engagement, and they can benefit from an already established network of startups, venture capitalists, service companies, other corporations, and experts that can help their activities. Plug and Play is an example of such an open innovation platform that serves as an aggregator of technology interests and challenges from many major corporations in a given vertical. The platform ensures that startups have the opportunity to meet the corporate decision-makers and facilitate matchups between corporations and startups for many industry verticals. For the participating startups, it is a free acceleration program—as the corporate memberships mostly sponsor it—that provides many opportunities for pilots, growth, and investments. For corporations, it provides a model where they can decrease the innovation risks and the resources needed to source startups and new technologies, while it increases their visibility toward early-stage startups that they can validate via pilot programs.

Typically, corporations use a mixture of these innovation models combining both internal and external programs. In the end, success comes when there is a good collaboration between these internal and external initiatives and proper alignment between the innovation front-end and back-end. Again, excellent execution of the opportunities identified is critical and one of the most significant challenges, especially when internal and external resources are involved. Investments and acquisitions (M&A) are another way to fuel corporate innovation. This section did not cover this type of innovation model, as the objectives of investments and M&As can be very diverse, such as acquiring intellectual property, bringing new talent on board, or gaining financial power.

## 9.7. CHARACTERISTICS OF MODERN CORPORATE INNOVATION LEADERS

The burden of leading change lies on the shoulders of the corporate leadership team. It is the role of the leadership team to make innovation part of the corporate culture. In today's fast-paced world, adaptability and collaboration are two of the most critical leadership traits. It is up to corporate leaders to set the tone and to lead by example to create an innovative culture, where innovation is encouraged and teams are empowered by delivering a clear and consistent message that inspires and motivates. A modern leader does not call all the shots but trusts the team to make the right decisions. Promoting innovation often requires leaders to take a step back and encourage employees to express their ideas and act on them.

Other characteristics of a modern corporate innovation leader include thinking fast, making effective decisions, and staying true to the company vision and strategy. With innovation comes failure, and the leadership team should convey optimism and a positive attitude while maintaining the targets to be pursued and supporting innovation. Great innovation leaders also tend to excel at risk management and have a good sense for new business opportunities. They lead with courage and exhibit curiosity.

As embracing diversity is essential for innovation, leaders who understand its power tend to do better than the ones who don't. Diversity in gender, age, ethnicity, culture, and skills leads to outstanding and modern organizations and provides a competitive edge, by bringing a variety of perspectives.

Finally, the modern innovation leader communicates openly, is authentic, and is culturally sensitive. By being people-centered, the leader contributes to a positive and happy culture which fosters innovation. While it is difficult to find leaders exhibiting all the traits described above, there is a strong correlation between these traits and the thriving modern innovation leaders.

## 9.8. CORPORATE VENTURING MODELS

Corporate venturing is not new. Historically, corporate venturing, as illustrated by an entity such as Intel Capital, focused on creating strategic partnerships with startups to help corporations augment their capabilities and reduce technology uncertainties in areas where the corporations have little to no experience. It makes sense when the corporation has some well-defined business or technical problems that partnerships can solve. A business unit generally drives it, but it is a stand-alone effort that is usually not disruptive enough and mostly incremental. However, today, value shifts occur at the intersection of industries. Corporations realize that they need to use corporate venturing to discover innovative products with different business models, and they need to do this with increasing speed. Business model innovation is taking center stage, and corporations need to adapt/extend their core business through digital transformation, new products, new services, or new operating models.

These days corporate venturing plays an increasing role in fueling the innovation engine of large corporations. By focusing on non-incremental innovation, corporate venturing is becoming a tool to explore innovative and disruptive opportunities. One of the goals of corporate venturing is to collaborate with startups to jointly explore new areas including business model innovation, instead of just swallowing the new startup which constrains the partnership output by the vision and execution capabilities of an internal business unit. The collaboration needs to be part of the strategic vision of the corporation to succeed, but with enough independence to be able to pull the corporation toward new destinations. For the corporate venturing unit, this includes a combination of a strategy aligned with that of the entire corporation, entrepreneurialism, collaboration, and risk capital.

Another emerging model for corporate venturing, illustrated in *Figure 9.6*, is to accelerate startups by leveraging corporate resources, such as marketing, channels to market and legal to add customer and operational value or capital, while startups bring value including expertise, talents, and technologies to the table. Some of the means, such as pilots, allow the corporation to be adaptive while decreasing the risk as compared to experimenting alone. In this role, corporate venturing needs to identify new opportunities—which are often difficult to source internally—spread its bets and resources toward different types of projects, and create strategic alignment with the corporate vision hoping for success along the way.

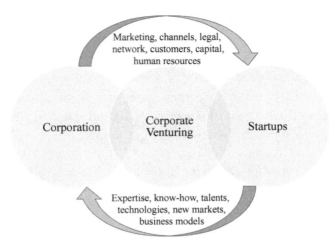

*Figure 9.6: The modern corporate venturing model.*

Finally, some corporations are now looking not only for strategic partnerships but rather for both strategic and financial value. For example, in April 2017 Panasonic announced an initial $100M fund for a California-based unit called Panasonic Ventures to access new business models, products, and services. The objective of this unit, while continuing to build strategic partnerships with internal groups, is to achieve profitable and sustainable commercial activity (in other words, make money).

There are more and more Corporate Venture Capital (CVC) activities. While in the past corporations ran CVC programs on average for two and a half years, today the average length of a CVC program operation is close to four years. CVC is also expanding geographically. While the majority of CVC investment is still in the United States, investments in European and Chinese startups are growing.

In the end, the role of corporate venturing is to translate customer needs and new technologies into a profitable and sustainable business model by aligning the corporate vision and resources with that of external startups. More than quick financial wins, CVC is powering long-term goals and strategy to support the current and future corporation ecosystem.

## 9.9. INCORPORATING DIGITAL TRANSFORMATION AND ITS RELATIONSHIP WITH INNOVATION

For many corporations, digital transformation (Herbert, 2017), which is the process of integrating digital technology at some level in the company, has become a top strategic priority. However, many companies are not structured to fit the digital reality, and their employees may need to change to adopt the digital mindset which is generally quicker and more iterative than what they have been used to in the past. It is one of the reasons why many more traditional companies fail at digitally transforming themselves, as it requires a change of the company culture, agility, and a good understanding of customers. Some of the companies sometimes realize that they have no choice and need to transform themselves, but they are too slow and get disrupted. A relevant example of such a company is Kodak, who failed to embrace fast enough the digital print wave. Generally, to succeed, companies need to restructure to change the way they are making decisions, how they interact with customers, and how they understand their needs.

When proceeding with digital transformation, companies are faced with competing priorities due to their finite amount of resources and time before they get disrupted. On the one hand, they still want to innovate their traditional model to maintain their competitiveness in the area they are operating in, and on the other hand, they want to transform themselves to enable new capabilities in the future. When not competing, digital transformation and innovation happen sequentially. It is rare for them to cooperate as the company is not prepared and structured to handle both at the same time.

Digital transformation and innovation are not mutually exclusive. *Figure 9.7* shows that digital technology value enables digital transformation and innovation. Digital transformation tends to be driven by short-term goals (e.g., productivity, or efficiency) while innovation tends to have a long-term orientation unless it is incremental. However, top company executives are often choosing one over the other as digital transformation can be a way to go toward future business. In both cases, it is essential to understand what the company wants to achieve, and to have a clear vision, focus, and scope for each initiative. Ideally, because time is of the essence, innovation should build on what digital transformation is providing, though it is always a good idea to have an innovation portfolio focused on improving the traditional business and at the same time creating the future. Driving this change is the role of the executive management team as it is directly related to the culture of the company. However, this is often easier said than done.

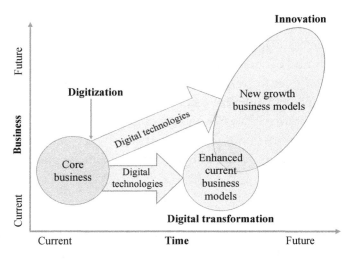

*Figure 9.7: Digital technology enables digital transformation and innovation.*

## 9.10. THE ENTREPRENEUR INNOVATOR TEAM

When you start a business, it is vital to find the right team members. If we look at successful companies, some common characteristics cannot be ignored, especially in the composition of the founding team. Many successful companies have a founding team composed of an entrepreneur and an innovator. For example, Steve Jobs paired with Steve Wozniak at Apple Computer, Bill Gates with Paul Allen at Microsoft, and Elon Musk with JB Straubel at Tesla. Both innovation and entrepreneurship skills are needed to be successful. Though some individuals operate as both innovator and entrepreneur, any successful company needs an individual or a team with at least these two skills. An innovator is a person who invents new technology, products, services, or processes. The innovator is the creative mind in the company who has some insights about doing something unique, not done before. It is, generally, not the person in charge of raising funds and leading the company. In contrast, an entrepreneur is driven by what it takes to make stuff happen against all the odds (e.g., raising money, convincing people). Entrepreneurs figure out how to get innovation adopted and what it takes to make it after the finish line. The gift of an entrepreneur is to reframe things continually and to turn rejection into an invitation. In every founding team, you want to have a person who can secure financing and stay in business as running out of money is one of the main reasons startups fail. Being a good leader is also essential as being able to influence and convince people of the company's vision and the ability to execute even in front of the most significant challenges is paramount. *Figure 9.8* highlights the key attributes of the entrepreneur and the innovator.

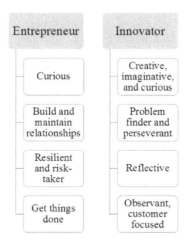

*Figure 9.8: Key attributes of the entrepreneur and the innovator.*

In a corporation, innovation and innovators are present. Many people are creative, have insights about new business opportunities, and are developing unique capabilities. What is often missing is the entrepreneur. A corporation does not have a function that is responsible for entrepreneurship. It is one of the significant challenges of modern corporation leaders in the 21$^{st}$ century, along with how to sustain entrepreneurship within large companies. However, we can wonder if a corporate entrepreneur will ever exist as incentives, autonomy, risks, and rewards are quite different from that found in a startup. It can probably exist but in a different way. It is something that corporations need to figure out. It depends on the corporate structure and how existing business and new business should interact. In a corporation, your role matches a job description, and there are precise requirements for each position. It creates an execution mindset. However, an entrepreneur has a learning and delivery mindset, which is very different. Entrepreneurship is mostly a calling, driven by passion. Entrepreneurs have reality distortions, and entrepreneurship is not a job defined by a job description!

It is difficult for corporations to be better than external disruptors. It is due to culture, structure, and process. To deal with these challenges, corporations must:

- Incentivize external resources.
- Acquire external innovators and entrepreneurs (e.g., Google acquired Android to penetrate the mobile space).
- Quickly copy innovators, though this also necessitates a deep understanding of customer needs to be successful.

Corporations revert to the above as they often have trouble disrupting themselves. It is what they need to figure out, as corporations have to innovate continuously to survive in the modern hypercompetitive world. Attracting, nurturing, retaining, and incentivizing entrepreneurs, and a good understanding and implementation of ambidexterity are some of the keys toward long-term success.

## 9.11. ESTABLISHING AN END-TO-END INNOVATION PIPELINE IS KEY TO CORPORATE INNOVATION SUCCESS

One of the main reasons for corporations failing to innovate is the lack of connection between innovation teams and their parent organization. Because of this disconnection, when innovative prototypes or other creative business opportunities are brought forward by innovation teams, the core of the organization is not ready to receive them. Furthermore, because in corporations year to year planning takes center stage, there is often no resource available to consider new opportunities if not planned. Corporations need to understand that:

- Innovation is likely to fail, if not connected from the start to innovation delivery.
- Inside the corporation, the innovation organization should be a delivery organization (or be connected to one) and not an organization in charge of delivering prototypes or demonstrations. It is crucial to connect innovation to its delivery and to define an end-to-end innovation pipeline, as shown in *Figure 9.9.*

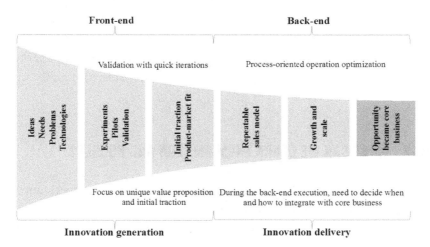

*Figure 9.9: The innovation pipeline.*

In a corporation, it is often the case that there is not one process or one organization responsible for this end-to-end innovation pipeline. Innovation usually starts at one place, inside or outside the corporation, and moves through all the challenges and roadblocks that are encountered one after the other without having anticipated any of them. The result is that most of the time, innovation dies as it takes too much time or stops before reaching the market. It is the responsibility of the executive management team to build a program that results in end-to-end outcomes that matter to them. It requires them to adapt the way innovations are generated and delivered. It has to start with leadership, culture, and well-defined end-to-end process flow.

A corporation often confuses motion with meaningful action and delivery. It is not a people problem as corporations are full of talented, innovative, and entrepreneurial people, but it is mainly about putting a process in place that connects the initial stage of innovation with its delivery to the market. A corporation needs to have a mindset, a physical space, and a process linked with market delivery for disruptive innovation to happen. Innovative projects that reach the market are no longer about business plan building and moving the opportunity from one internal team to another one. It is a team-based effort that has to be experiential, based on learning (hypothesis-testing) and focused on execution and market delivery. Concentrating on market delivery also means that corporations need to be able to quickly kill zombie projects which never die.

## 9.12. WHAT CAN WE LEARN FROM AMAZON AND GOOGLE?

Amazon has emerged as a new model of innovation effectiveness. Similarly, Google has been breaking new grounds in several areas (e.g., autonomous cars) with different degrees of success. What do these two companies have in common, and what can we learn from them?

Both Google and Amazon are using their profit engines (e.g., for Amazon, AWS and, to a certain degree, e-commerce though it is less profitable than AWS; and for Google, online search) to fund disruptive moonshots. They can afford to pump billions into disruptive projects year after year. Amazon and Alphabet's core business (Alphabet is Google's parent company) is so profitable that it allows these companies to fund many disruptive upstarts. This is to a point where other companies cannot compete as few companies have the cash to venture into moonshots that can disrupt, transform, or create a whole new industry. A company like Waymo, owned by Google and developing autonomous cars, was founded close to a decade ago, and still doesn't generate any profit. The profitability of Amazon and Google's core business and what it enables them to do for new business creation is a massive advantage to look for disruption in some new areas.

If we look at the Google innovation model, it is evident that Google has been keeping the pipeline of innovation going by empowering its employees and creating an environment where ideas can percolate. This environment, such as Google Cafés or the 20%-time policy, is encouraging creativity and interactions between employees and across teams while allowing Google to tap into the many talents of its employees. By cultivating a creative and passionate workforce, Google has been able to unleash the power of innovation from its employees. Other factors strongly influenced Google's success, including:

- Hiring generalists who are problem-solvers, not specialists, allowing the company and its employees to adapt to new areas, favoring intelligence and adaptability over experience.
- An emphasis on data, on setting high expectations, and on measuring progress. The focus on data facilitates decision-making and encourages experimentation. At Google, small teams come up with new ideas, demonstrate proof-of-concepts, and iterate.
- Innovation is the rule and not the exception. By creating this expectation across the organization, Google enables its

employees to innovate in areas where Google would not have imagined to innovate.

- Creating platforms that allow others to innovate such as Google Maps or Android. Google has been cultivating a community of thousands of developers providing additional brainpower and innovation.

On the other hand, the Amazon innovation model drives innovation from the top, and the company has progressively defined a set of guidelines and principles which have emerged as an excellent example of innovation effectiveness, disrupting industry after industry from bookselling to e-commerce and Web services. Amazon's success is due to several innovation practices, including:

- Customer-obsessed innovation powered by customer data providing a clear picture of the opportunities and allowing for driving innovation faster. A new project always starts with the customer. For Amazon, customers, and customer data are in the driver's seat.
- Ambitious goals, clear thinking, and risk-taking culture. At Amazon, new opportunities need to be scalable and have the potential to provide a significant return on capital. New opportunities are challenged by many in the company, providing some level of creative tension, which helps decision-making.
- First-mover principle, always experiment and fail fast. Many new Amazon initiatives (e.g., Kindle, Smart Speakers, AWS, or Amazon Go) disrupted industries, though when these areas started, Amazon did not have prior business experience. These examples show how Amazon has been willing to innovate, to take risks, and to learn via experimentation until they got these new products right.
- A continuous flow of ideas and lifelong learning, starting from the top (Amazon CEO, Jeff Bezos) guided by a culture built around an opportunity mindset and recognizing and embracing new trends quickly. In Amazon, ideas are assets.

This quick review of some of Google and Amazon's innovation practices is far from being exhaustive. In the end, their success is not only linked to one or several innovation practices but rather to innovation cultures, processes, and methodologies that go beyond a particular product or innovation and allow these companies to innovate continually. Given the success of these two companies, it is evident that they have been doing some things right. While there is not only one way to innovate, understanding where the success of these two very successful companies come from can help others derive their own best practices. These practices always need an adaptation to the changes that are continuously happening around us, and the society transitions to be successful. Google and Amazon have been very good at taking advantage of the Internet era and digital transformation to build tremendously successful companies that now allow them to venture into some new areas that they never thought they would pursue.

# CHAPTER 10

## The Future Innovation Landscape Powered by Data and AI

## 10.1. DATA IS AN ASSET AND INSIGHTS ARE THE NEW GOLD

As the volume of data available is increasing very rapidly, it is becoming a compelling asset for companies as it allows them to be results-driven and to find out what works and what does not. It also enables companies to improve their programs and organization to allocate resources more effectively. However, data is not very helpful until you extract meaning and insight from it. As shown in *Figure 10.1*, it is the insights that provide your company the means to make decisions, take actions, and drive growth. Many companies have more data at their fingertips than they can reasonably use, but insights remain relatively rare. The quality of data is also crucial as garbage input leads to garbage output. Being able to derive reliable models is fundamental. If the input data is noisy, outdated, or biased, then models will not be accurate. More and more data will have an impact on business growth. Companies like Google, Amazon, and Facebook have demonstrated how collecting data about their customers could enhance their business.

As data and the derived insights are becoming a key to business success, companies need to learn how to store and handle personal data and maintain data privacy. It must be part of the company's culture, and it is an essential area of focus for the wellbeing of the company. Everybody in the company needs to understand how to handle private data, what data is necessary and relevant to the company's business, how to use it, and how long it should be accessible and stored for. It includes obtaining customer consent when needed and implementing security measures to protect the data.

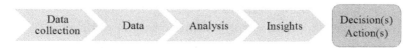

*Figure 10.1: Insights are the drivers for decision-making and a key to business success.*

As digital transformation is taking place, data and analytics can be used as a springboard for innovation and are becoming an engine for growth. Data is now available in orders of magnitude different to what companies had access to in the past including, for retailers such as Amazon, a precise knowledge of every consumer touchpoint. This data helps make more profitable decisions, as it allows companies to understand customers better, and make decisions faster, in some cases, nearly real-time. Many companies are realizing the power of big data and analytics, as it is driving better decisions. Data scientists are exploiting this data by developing smart technologies which can produce actionable insights.

Data is also the foundation of Artificial Intelligence (AI), machine learning, and deep learning. As these three terms will be used many times in this chapter, it is essential to understand the distinctions between them. AI is related to the incorporation of human knowledge into machines. Whenever a computer can complete tasks using a set of rules or algorithms that were generally performed by humans, such intelligent behavior is known as AI. Machine learning refers to computer systems that can "learn" from data. It enables machines to learn by themselves, using the provided data, and to make accurate predictions. It is one set of techniques to implement AI. Deep learning is a set of algorithms that are making use of artificial neural networks to perform machine learning (LeCun, Bengio, & Hinton, 2015). Artificial neural networks are inspired by how the information is processed in the human brain and somewhat imitate the way the human brain makes decisions. *Figure 10.1* illustrates the relationship between these different algorithms, as explained above.

AI, machine learning, and deep learning are only as good as the quality of the data that these algorithms are using. If the data is noisy and varies a lot, a data scientist has to spend a lot of time and effort to normalize (if need be), "clean," and curate this data so that it can be used to build reliable models. To be able to train models, data scientists should also ensure that they have enough useful data so that they can provide reliable insights toward the problem that they are trying to solve. Besides the amount of data, data scientists also need to make sure that they have access to all the data variables that are impacting their use case. It sometimes necessitates the collection of data from a variety of devices and systems and then a recombination of this data into a format that is suitable for a machine learning algorithm. While this may sound complicated, automatic algorithms in charge of pre-processing the data can generally do this. Adopting AI and machine learning algorithms is a journey that starts with data gathering, the creation of large data sets, which in many cases have ground truth associated with the data, and the building of advanced AI and machine learning models. Machine learning is an engine; the data is the fuel.

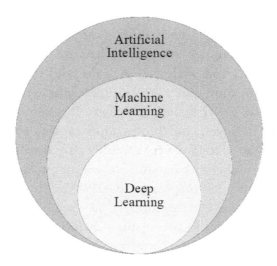

*Figure 10.2: The relationship between artificial intelligence, machine learning, and deep learning.*

## 10.2. DATA IS BECOMING THE DIFFERENTIATOR IN THE MARKET PLACE

Many companies are turning to the use of data to transform their business in the digital age. Digital information is slowly becoming the lifeblood of the enterprise, going from being collected, stored, and primarily ignored to becoming a strategic asset that needs to be governed and managed. By analyzing and interpreting data into easy to understand information, companies are leveraging business intelligence that effectively brings value to their organizations and drives better decisions. Companies are collecting data from diverse sources, both internally and externally, and are unleashing the power of machine learning and artificial intelligence. However, one of the challenges of data-driven organizations is to make sure that they are obtaining high-quality, well-curated data before sending it to their analytics engine, as otherwise, they will not reap the benefit of using this data. When it comes to implementing AI, it is all about data.

Another challenge is to implement processes and procedures to treat the data. Many remember the 50 million users affected by Facebook's data breach. So, customers want to understand how companies are securing their data and what they will do with it. This particular aspect is becoming more and more a differentiator in the marketplace, and the subject of government regulations. Businesses need to track and trace the life cycle and propagation of data throughout the company. They need to look very carefully after their customer data, gain their trust, and ensure compliance with regulations such as the General Data Protection Regulation (GDPR) in Europe and HIPAA for healthcare in the United States. This use and management of the data and the effort to obtain high-quality data, together with technology innovation, help companies to differentiate themselves in the market.

*Figure 10.3* shows the main differences between a data-aware organization where data mainly supports decisions and a data-driven organization where data drives decision-making and is key to all the business aspects. There are several competitive advantages linked to becoming a data-driven organization. These include:

- The creation of a more stable and consistent organization as decisions are not dependent only on a few individuals but can be attributable to the data.
- Awareness and responsiveness as companies can use data in real-time (or nearly real-time) to be proactive and often to predict customer preference behaviors. Amazon has been doing an outstanding job at this, and it is one of their definite competitive advantages.
- Continuous feedback about customer preferences, what worked and what didn't, and their responses to your products and services.

- A market-driven approach based on the confidence in the decisions taken, supported by the data instead of opinions and guesses.
- The above advantages eliminate doubt and faith-based decisions while providing real-time adaptation to unseen conditions. It is necessary in today's world where companies cannot anticipate long in advance the moves that they need to make.

*Figure 10.3: Characteristics of a data-aware and data-driven organization.*

As data is becoming an essential component of companies' strategies, the more data, the better, especially for organizations working in areas such as machine learning and artificial intelligence. Cleaning, curating, and annotating data, which, as discussed above, is still necessary to obtain good results from learning algorithms, can be very time and resource consuming. To deal with this concern, the creation of synthetic data is gaining popularity and has the potential to accelerate the testing and validation of machine learning and AI algorithms. Synthetic data is data that has been algorithmically generated using a generative model so that it is as close as possible to the properties of data from real-world scenarios. Data scientists can leverage synthetic data to optimize time, cost, and risk while increasing the data space to perform a better validation of the algorithms. Synthetic data comes with the ground truth needed for machine learning to train or test algorithms. While the generation of synthetic data is one way to deal with a limited amount of data, it is also essential to notice that it still replicates specific properties of real data. The random behaviors associated with real data may not be present.

## 10.3. THE IMPORTANCE OF HAVING A DATA-DRIVEN CULTURE THAT CAN DRIVE DIGITAL TRANSFORMATION

As digital transformation takes place, data and analytics act as a springboard for innovation as well as an engine for growth. In today's world, it is impossible to transform a company without data, as data is a requirement to deliver digital services, measure their effectiveness, and come up with new improvements. Companies need to develop a proper infrastructure and processes to get the most value from the data collected and to ensure that data can be used widely in their organization. By developing an appropriate technology infrastructure to collect, manage, combine, and access data, companies can enhance their efficiency and effectiveness. One of the critical barriers to go over is to break the silos that could prevent the company from sharing data widely and from combining data from multiple sources. As a way to overcome this, it is critical to promote a culture that prioritizes data and analytics. A data-driven culture is an environment that takes advantage of the economic value of data and analytics by enabling a holistic data approach that can leverage the data available today and in the future. This cultural mindset is essential for real success.

As discussed in the previous sections, it is what you do with the data that matters. Besides tracking information such as employee assessment or productivity, data analysis can enable companies to figure out strategies that can extract the best of their employees by pointing out areas where employees excel and areas for improvements. Based on the data, managers can show their employees why they are making some decisions and why they follow specific strategies or directions. In the end, the data allows everyone to use facts to make sense of what is happening instead of relying on opinions and feelings.

Another area where data is changing the way companies have been operating is the launch of products and services. Digital transformation is often happening when companies desire to be more relevant to their customers. By understanding better their customers and gathering data across all departments about all the aspects related to the products and services (e.g., time to delivery, customer support), companies can now monitor their progress and be confident that they are heading in the right direction. They can control their costs, provide better customer service, accelerate their time to market, and optimize their resources.

The flow of data available is increasing at a tremendous pace, fueled by sensors and the Internet of Things (IoT) platforms that continuously collect and transmit data. IoT devices are exploding both for the consumer, and commercial and industrial areas. From wearable devices to autonomous cars and the sensing of industrial equipment to applications and enterprise software platforms allowing to monitor company initiatives, all activities and behaviors are being digitalized, setting up the stage for disruption. It is an exciting time, and the future belongs to companies who will be able to derive and implement a data strategy that will allow them to optimize their current activities and transform themselves to provide innovations to their customers. Data is the glue that can facilitate collaborations throughout your company as data combined with software can integrate different capabilities that used to be independent.

Digital transformation can create fear among employees, as many people may want to know what it means for their job security. However, a digital workplace enables employees to be more creative and innovative. As always, communication is crucial and, to succeed, every employee needs to be on board.

## 10.4. THE POTENTIAL CHALLENGES OF BIG DATA AND DATA-DRIVEN TRANSFORMATION

Data-driven transformation is attractive for many companies and, as mentioned in the previous sections, can be seen as an engine for growth. However, it is essential to be aware of some of the main challenges that companies may face when implementing it. *Figure 10.4* summarizes the most critical ones, while the list below provides more details on some aspects.

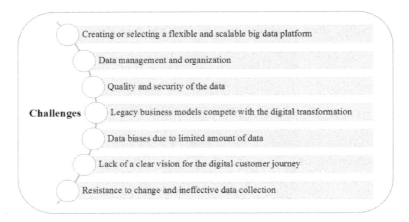

**Challenges**

- Creating or selecting a flexible and scalable big data platform
- Data management and organization
- Quality and security of the data
- Legacy business models compete with the digital transformation
- Data biases due to limited amount of data
- Lack of a clear vision for the digital customer journey
- Resistance to change and ineffective data collection

*Figure 10.4: The challenges of big data and data-driven transformation.*

- Creating a big data platform is not simple, and there is an inherent complexity to deal with, from collecting reliable data to quickly accessing it. Companies do not always understand what is needed when they jump into the big data bandwagon, and they can waste a lot of time and resources. Often, the generation of new data is happening quickly, and organizations can struggle to deal with the data volume in real-time. To start with big data, seeking professional help to get familiar with best practices is often the right way to go.
- Syncing data across a wide range of data sources and extracting information from the data requires excellent data management and organization process. Access to skills and talents are not always readily available. Today, there is a lack of data scientists

and, given the proliferation of data and machine learning, it is likely to continue for the foreseeable future.

- Reliability and security of the data are essential to consider. Big data is not 100% accurate, especially if it comes from different sources. So, spending some time and resources to improve data quality is essential. Security can also be a challenge, especially when dealing with large amounts of data among collaborators. The data itself needs to be securely protected, not only its access by the applications that are making use of it.

- Scalability is a requirement from the beginning as, when more data is available, scaling should happen without extra effort and reduced performance.

- Depending on the use case, making sure that the collected information does not have built-in biases is critical, as insights will reflect just what the data represents. Even the best machine learning and AI algorithms cannot change this.

- While data-driven transformation can be an objective, there may not be a clear vision of the customer benefits, as inexperience and lack of knowledge of the legacy business can get in the way of a new data-driven approach that is riskier at first and unproven.

Big data and analytics via machine learning or some other means can be compelling. However, companies should be cautious about how to execute and how to take advantage of digital transformation. It can be the difference between success and failure. Close to ten years ago, P&G aspired to being a highly digital company, but ran into some challenges, because it did not invest in digital in a targeted way. Another example is Hasbro. By leveraging data, Hasbro tailored its advertising efforts to meet the needs of its consumers and was successful at expanding sales.

## 10.5. THE PROMISES AND CHALLENGES OF THE AGE OF AI

The term Artificial Intelligence comes from the 1950s. However, it is really with the progress made by deep learning that it came to the forefront of research and that we have seen its power to perform tasks previously reserved to humans. Most of these tasks have to do with automation and making complex decisions as the dream of matching "human intelligence" is still far away. Most of the progress made in this area is mainly due to the amount of data and computation that is now available. If we take the example of deep learning, neural networks were applied to many tasks (e.g., speech recognition) more than 30 years ago. However, at that time, there was not enough data and computation available to build complex and flexible models that were able to generalize. AI is a compelling technology as it applies to many tasks. Today, many startups are using some form of AI in almost every field (e.g., surveillance, logistics, legal, medical diagnostic, robotics, inspection). When data is available, AI is a candidate to learn, optimize, and automate. Kai-Fu Lee, one of the pioneers of speech recognition and AI, even mentioned that "AI is going to change the world more than anything in the history of humankind. More than electricity." For businesses, embracing AI can bring considerable benefits from innovations to productivity and growth (Lee, 2018). For many industries, implementing AI is not a question of competitiveness but a matter of survival.

AI will transform many companies and create different types of business. Its impact on work is likely to be profound, and it will change dramatically many sectors of the economy such as healthcare, where AI applies to many areas such as prevention and risk assessment, detection and diagnostic, and patient triage. The demand for some skills will decrease while that for others will grow. AI is also making strides in areas such as preventive maintenance where AI can detect anomalies, autonomous driving where AI will progressively replace human drivers, logistics where AI helps to optimize the routing of deliveries and improve fuel efficiency or call centers where AI can improve call routing and product recommendations. The impact of AI in these areas and many others is on efficiency and productivity.

According to the McKinsey Global Institute's report published in December 2017 (McKinsey Global Institute, 2017), about 50% of current work activities are automatable. It is for these activities that the impact of AI is the greatest, with an emphasis on the ones that can be more easily automated. Most of the recent progress is due to advances in deep learning. For now, China and the United States are leading most AI-related activities. As AI is spreading to many applications, AI tools and platforms are becoming available, and data will become the differentiator in the marketplace.

As many tasks are likely to be automated using AI, there will be an increased demand for skills requiring a human touch, such as communication and empathy. For example, as AI is transforming the field of radiology by detecting cancers with high accuracy, radiologists will spend more of their time communicating, comforting, and empathizing with a patient, whereas currently most of their time is spent reading images. There will also be a greater need for critical higher cognitive skills, as AI is still far away from being able to approach humans for these tasks.

Though the promises of AI are numerous and AI will impact our society forever, we should not underestimate the challenges and current limitations of the technology. From a societal point of view, we need to address concerns about data privacy, misuse of AI, biases introduced by the data used for training the models, and how algorithms use this data. Another critical challenge is related to ethics. As now using AI machines can yield more complex decisions, some questions arise about who is accountable for those decisions and what the assumptions are that led to these decisions. For AI-enabled machines to support human decision-making, it is necessary to build trust, transparency, accountability, and to be able to explain how computers make decisions. From a technology point of view, some of the limitations include:

- Difficulties in gathering a large quantity of human-labeled training data, as today's algorithms require a lot of annotated data to provide excellent performance. Some efforts are underway to use synthetic data and noisy data which do not require human annotation. However, these efforts are still at the research level. On the other hand, a technique, called "transfer learning," where scientists can train a model for a specific task and reuse it for a similar activity has been promising to solve the challenge brought by a limited amount of data. In many ways, the objective is to be able to learn more from less.

- Lack of generalization outside of the training data. As current AI systems operate in a relatively narrow knowledge space, they do not have a good understanding of our world, and do not deal very well with the context.
- Some AI algorithms, such as deep learning, are often used as a black box which takes data as input and outputs some decisions. It creates an "explainability" problem, as it becomes difficult to explain what the factors are which led to the decision made.

*Figure 10.5* summarizes some of the promises and challenges of AI, along with some of the limitations discussed above.

The AI field is progressing very quickly, and much data is being collected to feed the progress made in machine learning. It is only the beginning of the journey, and the potential is enormous. On the other hand, there are also legitimate concerns. Both AI technology and its social implications need to progress at the same time to create a better world.

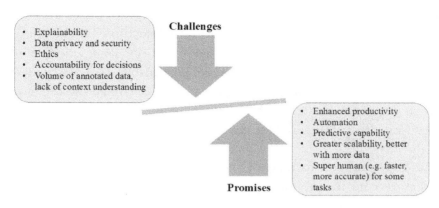

*Figure 10.5: The promises and challenges of AI.*

## 10.6. AI AND DATA-DRIVEN COMPUTING

For many years, Moore's law, predicting that the number of transistors that can fit into a chip will double every 18-24 months, has been driving technology achievements. However, after several decades of tremendous growth, we are at the end of this period. On the other hand, every two years, we are creating more data than the data generated in all of history so the computing power to process this data cannot keep up. The availability of data and machine learning is also introducing a new way of solving problems. The traditional way to solve problems is still to develop algorithms that have been designed to perform a specific task. The difference is that with machine learning, training the artificial neural networks is replacing the design and the programming of the algorithm. To be able to process more and more data faster, AI chips, which are designed to perform matrix computation very quickly, are being developed. AI is dramatically changing many computing paradigms of the 1990s and 2000s, as new architectures and hardware solutions are progressively being proposed to speed up computation. More advanced linear algebra solutions embedded in hardware and taking advantage of parallel computation are becoming part of the AI innovation landscape. It will transform our computing infrastructures. Edge computing, where complex processing is done at the edge and in real-time before communicating with a central processing node, is becoming a trend (see *Figure 10.6* for the advantages of edge and cloud computing). In other words, computing architectures are changing, as, in the new AI era where you have to process large amounts of data quickly, current solutions are not sustainable. In a distributed architecture, such as the one in *Figure 10.6,* edge computing can deal with requirements such as low latency, application autonomy, data security, data privacy, and limited bandwidth.

As data continues to increase, it will be more and more difficult to store data in one place. Data will have to be distributed and processed by a distributed architecture which will have a network of nodes that will become smarter and smarter. The traditional model of a data center will change as data centers will likely not be able to accommodate the needs placed on these centers by the pace of the data increase. It is compounded by the needs of our modern society for real-time communication anytime, anywhere, and the continuous decrease of the information life cycle. Businesses will become more and more competitive if they can process data in real-time (or nearly real-time) and use the insights to deliver instant value. A new era of computing, driven by AI, is coming, where data will be used innovatively by advanced computing architectures. This new era will be data-driven and new computing architectures will be able to process a massive amount of unstructured data.

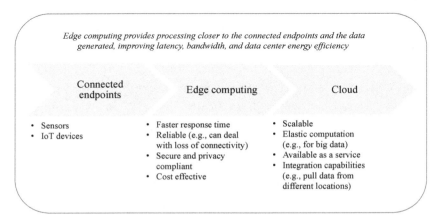

*Figure 10.6: Advantages of edge and cloud computing.*

## 10.7. CAN AI SURPASS HUMAN CAPABILITIES?

It is not a surprise that computers can do very well at repetitive tasks and solving problems that involve much data. Humans are not well suited to do the same things repetitively as we get bored, distracted, and prone to errors. The machine brings reliability and consistency, and as more and more computing power is available, computers can process a large amount of information and detect patterns in data that humans cannot comprehend. For these types of tasks, it is clear that AI-powered machines can surpass human capabilities. Among the roughly 50% of today's activities that can benefit from automation, there are many types of tasks, including:

- Organizing and sorting information.
- Playing games where rules are well understood.
- Driving cars better than humans (not proven yet, but the future is going in this direction).
- Detecting anomalies from images where these anomalies are not even visible to a human eye and identifying abnormal behaviors.
- Translating a text into many languages.

For these tasks where the ambiguity is limited, AI can do exceptionally well as it can help increase speed, efficiency, or safety. As soon as the ambiguity increases and that context and nuances come into play, it is much more difficult for AI to provide performance that even approaches human capabilities. When the ambiguity is high, or tasks are socially or cognitively driven, humans are much faster, more accurate, and more reliable. Humans can learn unlimited patterns and then select the ones they need to apply depending on the situation/context. Humans are also very skilled at inferring something new and being creative when faced with challenges and new unseen problems. AI is still limited by what the algorithms have seen before during the training phase.

As data is more and more available, and researchers have access to more and more computing power, AI will become increasingly influential. However, there is still a very long way before AI can rival humans for tasks that include ambiguity and creativity. We are moving toward a world where AI will collaborate with humans without replacing humans, augmenting human capabilities and allowing humans to spend more time doing what they are experts at, which is dealing with other people. We should embrace the advantages that AI provides in terms of superhuman capabilities and, while making sure that we control in some ways the applications of AI, we should use AI to improve the world for current generations and generations to come. The future that many of us are envisioning is a future where technology and AI are becoming a part of our world, seamlessly integrated into the background instead of separated. It is a future where AI is augmenting human beings to make the most out of human beings and to amplify our unique capabilities.

## 10.8. THE FUTURE OF AI AND THE AI-DRIVEN ECONOMY OF ABUNDANCE

Digital transformation and AI are going to impact every single industry and everything we do. At a macro level, areas such as sustainability, energy, healthcare, security and safety, and transportation are ripe to be disrupted by smarter and smarter algorithms. It will allow these industries to save money and provide new value (see *Figure 10.7,* which is illustrating some areas that digital transformation and AI are impacting or will disrupt in the not so distant future). The possibilities are infinite. Here is a glimpse at what the future holds for us in the next decade:

- Drones and robots will increase our security by providing access to areas which were too life-threatening to reach before. They will also allow automating monitoring and inspection tasks, making our world safer.

- AI will enable access to better healthcare as it will augment human doctors' capabilities and will allow them to focus their energy on improving the wellbeing of their patient. This will happen not only via better diagnostics and assistance but by enhancing the communication with their patients and their emotional wellbeing. Besides, AI will allow improving illness prevention by detecting early signs of diseases and enabling doctors to take actions while still in an early stage of the disease progression.

- As the energy grid is getting digitalized and cities too via smart city initiatives, AI will impact climate change, environmental issues, transportation, and more generally, sustainability. Urban planning and infrastructure monitoring are two areas that will be positively impacted by AI progress.

- New AI-based products and services will be created, such as products for the elderly population to provide better care but also to compensate for the decrease in their physical and cognitive capabilities.

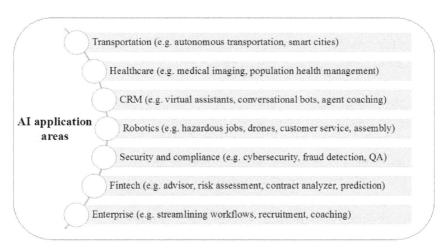

*Figure 10.7: Promising AI applications.*

Today, some applications, such as chatbots for customer service or robotics for manufacturing, are already used widely. There are currently many activities in motion where advances will undoubtedly happen in the next decade. However, AI will reach far beyond these areas and, indeed, will transform our lives. To do so, it will be important that the companies making use of AI build trust with their customers, as these new capabilities cannot happen without trust. Customers want to know that the results provided by AI can be trusted and that companies act in their best interest as they want to have control over their information and its usage. Trust always has been and will continue to be a business imperative and key to sustainable growth. Ethics, mentioned earlier, will also increasingly be at the center of AI activities, as AI will not be able to ignore the societal implications enabled by the changes created.

AI progress will likely be exponential as the availability of data is increasing very rapidly, the level of investment in AI is sky-rocketing, and the quality and cost of sensors are improving very quickly. Digital transformation and AI are likely to create a new economy of abundance (Diamandis, 2012), driven by the convergence of renewable energy, autonomous transportation, and digital communication, instead of being driven by oil, automobiles and wire-based telecommunications. Our current economy is driven mainly by resource scarcity (e.g., fossil fuel). If we continue in this direction, we will be destroying ourselves little by little, building products that cannot decompose or be reused and, consequently, not decreasing our carbon emission. In this new economy, data, software, and machine learning are essential, and it drives down the cost of new products and services. AI is powering a more automated world that captures knowledge and processes through data and software and is moving us from an economy of scarcity to an economy of abundance, as illustrated by the sharing economy and companies such as Uber and Airbnb. Many industries will experience a disruption, and the transition is likely to be painful as many jobs will be displaced and replaced by machines that will free us from repetitive and dangerous activities and push us toward tasks that make humans human. For many people, especially the millennial generation, access is becoming more important than ownership, as sustainability and fairness are becoming their guiding principles. It is a very different world where participation and sharing in networks is empowering, and isolation is a problem. By embracing AI, people and businesses will be more prepared to ride the transition and succeed in this new economy.

## 10.9. PREPARING YOUR CULTURE FOR AI

There are things that AI can do very well, such as detecting patterns, and some things that are still very challenging for AI, such as relating to humans as humans do. The success of AI is strongly dependent on how it fits with the tasks at hand and how it integrates into the organization's culture as well as the appetite of the organization for change. One of the questions often asked is: How do we foster the right AI culture? Success will come by adopting a new way of thinking and a mindset that can leverage AI. As we already mentioned, one of the keys to leveraging AI is to choose a data-driven strategy, as AI-based decisions get better with more data since AI-based systems can continuously learn from data. At the core, leveraging AI starts by building a culture of data and evidence-based decision-making. It includes:

- Promoting a culture of learning and continuous monitoring through experimentation, testing, and validation. It is essential to be agile, to experiment, and to course-correct if required.
- Measuring and recording everything as data will allow you to make better decisions and to progress. The following sentence reflects quite well Google's strategy in this respect: "If you cannot measure it, you cannot improve it."
- Making all the information available to all employees so that information can flow. It will enable employees to make decisions, to be part of the change and build on top of the information collected.

Besides creating a data-driven culture, it is also essential to create a company vision for AI so that the organization can adopt a new way of thinking early and be prepared. AI is likely to transform any business, and having a shared company vision that is closely related to the company strategy helps bring everybody onto the same page and set priorities. Finally, creating a positive track record can help to align employees with the benefits that AI can bring. It helps to build trust in embracing AI at the organization level. At first, AI may threaten the existence of some businesses, but successful transformation leveraging AI can provide big wins.

## 10.10. DIGITAL INNOVATION POWERED BY AI

With the quick evolution of AI, it is essential to understand that very soon it will be everywhere. However, this also implies that the competitive advantage that AI provides can also vanish very quickly. On average, the age of a company on the S&P 500 decreased from 60 years around the 1950s to less than 20 years today. It raises the question about how to stay relevant in the age of AI.

Digitization is everywhere. However, it is clear that adoption is very uneven across companies, e.g., healthcare and construction are two industries contributing significantly to our GDP, but digitization is still lagging in them. Companies that are leading digital innovation such as Google, Apple, Amazon, and Facebook have faster revenue growth and higher productivity than less digitized companies. AI and automation activities will stimulate more digital transformation effort and enable productivity growth across the entire economy. It is necessary because due to demographic effects, such as aging and falling birth rates, growth will inevitably fall, and digital innovation will be required to increase and sustain economic growth.

Accelerating progress in AI and automation now brings a broader range of possibilities for users, businesses, and more generally, the economy. The emergence of IoT and the ability to capture and analyze large volumes of data can help companies streamline their operations in ways that were not possible before. Digital innovation is enabling business models and capabilities that are reshaping industries, such as retail, insurance, transportation, banking, and manufacturing. Intelligent automation and the rise of cloud computing is enabling small companies to disrupt many sectors using fewer resources as compared to the ones used in the past. As an example, in the area of finance, open banking is enabling, via Fintech APIs, third-party developers to come up with new applications and services (e.g., comparing competing products from different providers or giving consumers more financial choices) around the data obtained from financial institutions. It is a model that applies to many other industries. Data aggregation startups can take advantage of access to data to build the base layer for innovation.

The fast advancement of technology and digital innovation has made it necessary to change the business models of many industries, to rethink the way many companies interact with customers and to reorganize the structure of the company itself. A good example illustrating the changes that have been happening are the new business models for ridesharing and usage-based auto insurance. If we look at companies such as Lyft or Uber, automation has not only provided an acceleration of processes, but it also brought increased flexibility and customer convenience while changing the business model of asset ownership or employment relation. New digital products and services, such as ridesharing, are creating new, longer-term business opportunities, and new playing fields are opening up access to new customers and creating additional access to existing customers. *Figure 10.8* shows some important areas strongly impacted by digital innovation and AI. AI is leveraging the power of data to create new experiences, improve productivity, and develop innovative platforms to accelerate partnership development and reinvent how to do business.

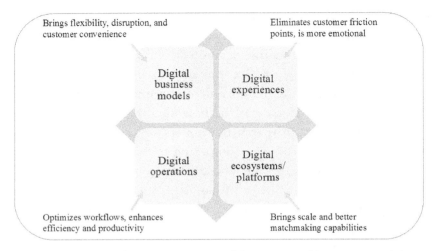

*Figure 10.8: Digital innovation powered by AI is enabling new capabilities.*

## 10.11. THE EVOLUTION OF MAN-MACHINE COLLABORATION IN THE AI ERA

In the previous chapters, we talked about the power of collaborative innovation. Digital innovation and tools such as messaging, video conferencing, or online platforms, have made human–human collaboration more accessible and more effective. Technological progress, such as the Internet, is bringing people together even when they are geographically separated. Another area which, in recent years, has evolved very quickly is man-machine collaboration. There is reasonable fear that AI may ultimately replace human jobs for many tasks throughout the economy. However, as AI is helping increase automation, its most significant impact will likely be in complementing and augmenting human capabilities, not replacing them.

So that people can take full advantage of AI and its power to augment their capabilities, they need to understand how to integrate AI and how processes need to be redesigned to support the collaboration. AI can do things that people cannot do, e.g., analyzing a large quantity of data or detecting hidden patterns not visible by humans, and inversely people's cognitive ability and creativity are unmatched by machines. By maximizing this collaboration, people and AI can enhance each other's strengths.

One of the promising areas is taking advantage of AI–human collaboration in the workplace where virtual assistants are currently interacting with millions of customers by answering frequently asked questions. If the system cannot resolve an issue, the customer request goes to a customer service representative who will help the customer, while the machine will learn from the interaction to deal better in the future with similar customer cases. This example shows how humans can focus on solving complex issues while automation can provide an effective way to handle most of the requests (about 70%), 24 hours a day, and seven days a week. AI and machine learning are increasingly penetrating the workplace for collaborative business workflows and processes to enable intelligent and more convenient experiences. It allows companies to make decision support systems smarter, and to increase speed and customer satisfaction.

It is clear that for many companies, the evolution of man-machine collaboration is a pathway to efficiency. "Superhuman" sensing or processing is enabling the collection of real-time insights that companies could not access in the past. People are still at the center of decision-making while machines provide new valuable insights that enable people to do a better job, to prioritize, and to focus on what they do best. As AI is getting smarter and is deployed in our lives, this "intelligent" collaboration will become more and more sophisticated, to contribute to a better world where humans will fully embrace and leverage their uniqueness.

# CHAPTER 11

## Learning from Past Experiences in the Corporate and Startup Worlds

### 11.1. BACKGROUND

This last chapter focuses on many personal experiences acquired from working in a large corporation and several startups in Silicon Valley. At first, it may appear as a collection of learnings or episodes that are disconnected, but the following sections represent some critical lessons learned that shaped this book and pushed me to spend the time to write it.

I started my career in France in a public research center ("CNRS") located inside a University (Université Henri Poincaré) in the northeast of France in a city called Nancy. It is where I started my research career while pursuing a Doctorate in Computer Science with a focus on speech recognition. In the middle of my Doctorate, I decided to go to the United States to perform some of my research, and what I thought initially would be a limited research experience transformed into more than 30 years, with a brief stay back in Nancy to finish and present my thesis. In a beautiful city called Santa Barbara, I did some research on speech recognition for an industrial research laboratory of Panasonic, and after roughly ten years, I was appointed to the direction of the laboratory. The mission of this Panasonic unit was to develop technology breakthroughs in speech processing and make use of the technology developed to create new business opportunities. In 2004, I was asked by Panasonic to go to Japan to lead the global speech activities of Panasonic distributed between China, Japan, and the United States. My stay in Japan ended in 2006 when I was asked to start the innovation activities of Panasonic in Silicon Valley and to leverage the Silicon Valley ecosystem to accelerate the Panasonic new business creation initiatives. In the course of these activities, I led the creation of an internal startup in the area of digital health which triggered the creation of a new North American business unit in the field of Health and Wellness. In 2015, I moved to the startup world, and since then have been involved with many startups and accelerators as a startup executive, advisor, entrepreneur in residence, or mentor. In the course of my career, I evolved from a technologist and computer scientist to an open innovation specialist with an emphasis on the creation of new business opportunities using collaborative innovation and partnerships. Inside Panasonic, I pioneered customer-focused approaches, such as design thinking and lean startup, and led the transformation of Panasonic innovation capabilities from a technology-based methodology to market- and customer-needs-focused methods to create new business. With startups, the emphasis has been on product-market fit, new business models, and international market expansion. During my experiences in the corporate and startup worlds, I have always been interested in finding new ways to deal with ever-changing challenges and to innovate better and faster with new approaches that would maximize the chances of success.

The front-end of innovation is generally well understood by both startups and corporations, though startups usually have a speed advantage as they are more agile and can be bolder with their decision-making. One of the difficulties that both startups and corporations face during the front-end of innovation is to reach a convincing product-market fit. The back-end of new business creation, which is how to scale and execute, is generally harder for startups as the process and the human resources needed for the execution often has to be put in place at the same time as growth is happening. For corporations, though experience for both the front-end and the back-end of innovation is generally available due to past successes, it is often hard to connect them as there is an existing business to protect and nurture that can get into the way of creating new business. The next sections are reflecting on my personal experiences and touch on some of these topics.

## 11.2. NEW BUSINESS CREATION LEVERAGING TECHNOLOGY BREAKTHROUGHS

I spent much time in my career developing breakthrough technologies in the area of speech recognition and, more generally, machine learning. In the 1980s and 1990s, Japanese companies such as Panasonic established research and development laboratories all across the United States, and they were aiming at long-term technology development as a way to create new business. The model was as follows:

- Become an expert and a leader in your field by being aware of technology advancements in your area, publish in international conferences, and participate in research events organized by the community.
- Patent the technology developed after making sure it provides value by comparing it to the work of other researchers in the field.
- Evaluate the benefits of the technology and integrate it into applications together with business divisions for products that they manufactured.

This approach generated many publications and patents but failed to create the business impact that Panasonic expected. The main reasons were as follows:

- The main objectives of the work done and the KPIs measured were related to the number of publications and patents filed.

The incentives used connected only loosely with business impact.

- Even when a competitive technology became available, the business divisions often did not know what to do with it as it was not developed to solve a particular problem.

- In many cases, the technology was still not good enough to solve a problem that would generate customer value at a cost that the market could accept.

- The business division was looking at the technology as an additional feature (incremental improvement) of an existing product instead of looking at it as a disruptive technology to create a new business.

- The business creation and technology development were disconnected, so it was challenging to convince a business division to adopt the technology as the potential business impact was unclear and not defined at the beginning of the technology development.

- It was still early for speech recognition and machine learning. The data available was scarce, and the computational power available was still too small to yield the accuracy that would make an application usable.

- As the technology was not yet mature, it took a long time to come up with technology that was unique and had a chance to make a practical impact.

In summary, with a very talented group of researchers, we published many articles, filed numerous patents, but we did not create much customer value as the technology was in search of a problem to solve. While today, the approach of many Japanese companies has changed mainly because the pace of innovation has accelerated, there is still a strong tendency for Japanese companies to focus on technology developed internally as a way to drive new business development. While the approach can create some isolated successes, and it is possible to develop technology faster than before by building on top of software or hardware building blocks which already exist, it is still very challenging to sustain this way to innovate. Today, a customer-first and market-first approach are the most appropriate and the faster way to reach the market and create value. Large corporations should develop a portfolio approach that combines internal technology developments, a collaborative and partnership strategy, and an evidence-based methodology to create new opportunities based on market and customer validation. Because of the speed at which new products are coming to market, it is not possible to dissociate business impact, technology developments, and customer needs. These three areas need to be considered and well understood at the initial stage of the project to increase your chances of success. Today, the success of voice assistants such as Siri from Apple, Alexa from Amazon, and Google Assistant is due to technological progress, but also to the facts that people are more open to trying new technologies, voice assistants are more affordable, and the deployed solutions are doing a better job at solving customer needs. Applications such as searching for an answer or listening to streaming music became popular because voice is a quick and natural way to perform these actions, and the cost of an error is low. Many challenges still exist, such as data privacy, but voice is on its way to becoming one of the primary interfaces with machines.

## 11.3. CREATING NEW BUSINESS BY LEVERAGING INTERNAL BUSINESS UNITS

In large corporations, business divisions and corporate R&D are different departments, each with its own goals and objectives. Typically, R&D comes up with new concepts and technologies and, when they are mature enough, pitches the new opportunities to the business units. Then, the business divisions decide whether these opportunities are worth exploring and if they want to get involved. However, given the fact that the divisions do not engage at the beginning of the opportunity creation process, the likelihood that they will engage later on is low, because the opportunity did not consider the business constraints. When R&D pitches the new opportunities to the business divisions, below are some of the likely scenarios, especially in the area on consumer products, which is an area I had much experience with:

- Cost is an issue, or technology is difficult to implement due to hardware constraints.
- The business unit does not have the bandwidth to dedicate to the new opportunity, and it needs to wait for a new planning cycle to have a chance to consider it.
- The opportunity is too disruptive or out of the scope of the business unit's current activities, so it cannot integrate into the existing new business creation pipeline.
- There is no expert in the business unit to lead the opportunity.
- The business unit is skeptical about the market for the new business and the value created, as it was not involved in the initial phase of the project, or it is not familiar with the opportunity area.

The points above show that a model where R&D and business development are two separate phases of the new business creation is prone to fail. At best, it is possible to develop incremental innovation or new features for existing products, but very rarely, this model succeeds in creating new opportunities that have a substantial impact on the company's bottom line. In the past, when the time to market was slower, it was possible to deal with some of the issues mentioned above and do a course correction. However, today, because of the fast innovation speed, it is not possible anymore. It is why, in many large corporations, the size of corporate R&D has been decreased significantly at the expense of some other new business creation schemes such as open innovation and collaborative innovation.

## 11.4. THE DEATH VALLEY BETWEEN THE CORPORATE FRONT-END AND BACK-END OF INNOVATION

As long as the front-end and the back-end of new business creation will be separated, there will be many new potential businesses that will fall into what I call the "Death Valley" of opportunities (see *Figure 11.1*). It is the place where projects fail to convince the top executive leadership that they are worth funding, and the corporate business units that it is worth investing resources in productizing the opportunity. It happens because the way to create a business based on the opportunity has not been planned or given enough thoughts. How to execute a business opportunity should be designed even before the project starts. Without having a good vision for the end-to-end process, the likelihood that the project will fail is very high. Instead, it is best to plan the life cycle of the project and a set of milestones that, if reached, will enable the project to proceed to the next stage. By not planning the entire life cycle of the project, there is no clear accountability for the new business to be created and at the end of each phase, there is a new battle to go to the next one. By defining a set of clear milestones and a possible execution path, it is easier to decide whether the project should continue or not.

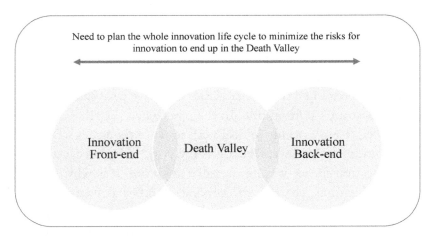

*Figure 11.1: The Death Valley of innovation is real when the end-to-end innovation process is not well planned.*

Another element related to the project life cycle that is contributing to the failing of many opportunities in a corporate environment is the yearly budget planning. The fact that corporations often do not see or do not want to commit beyond the annual budget plan is a significant issue as typically commitments are reset at the fiscal year boundary. It prevents innovation groups from adequately sustaining the development of an opportunity as budget fluctuations affect the team commitment and engagement adversely. Because of the yearly project cycle, and the lack of clear criteria to abandon or pursue an opportunity, projects tend to start, stop, or continue at the boundary of each fiscal year. It is quite different in the startup world as startups work typically on one opportunity and are fully committed to developing this opportunity, independently of each fiscal year boundary. Startups are more worried about running out of money than the beginning or end of their fiscal year.

In contrast to yearly budget planning, rolling forecasts (Stretch, 2012) aim for a constant adjustment of planning based on what is happening. They are an alternative to the traditional budgeting process. They are less rigid than the annual budget and can support the fluctuating nature of innovation and emerging business.

Even with R&D having significant resources, without a clear separation between technology development and the creation of new business opportunities, the Death Valley has been full of missed opportunities. In today's world, where the market and customer-centric approaches often lead new business creation, this is less the case than before. However, if corporations can do a better job at tackling the issues mentioned above, the likelihood of new business opportunities ending up in the Death Valley will significantly decrease.

## 11.5. AN INTERNATIONAL PERSPECTIVE AND SOME ESSENTIAL LEARNINGS FROM WORKING IN FRANCE, JAPAN AND IN THE UNITED STATES

For any business, being able to understand different cultures and gain an "international" viewpoint is critical for the following reasons:

- It is likely that internationalization/globalization will be required to grow your business.

- In today's world, people are more mobile, and the workforce is diverse and composed of people from different countries.
- The Internet era gave rise to possibilities that go beyond our geographic boundaries, for example, when exploring opportunities such as outsourcing or partnerships.

I was lucky enough to be able to work on three different continents and to work with colleagues from different countries. Through those experiences, I learned how to appreciate cultural differences along with how to adapt to doing business in different countries (France, Japan, and the United States). The points below summarize some essential information that I learned over the years. These points represent my personal "boots-on-the-ground" experiences, and one should avoid overgeneralizing too much. However, I believe that they provide some hints to entrepreneurs about things that they need to pay attention to, and many of you will likely be able to relate your own experience.

- In the United States, it is essential to engage quickly with potential customers or partners. Otherwise, they may think that you are not interested or professional. It tends to be different in other countries, particularly in France, where people often do not have the same sense of urgency as in the United States.
- In the United States, marketing uses data and measurable metrics to understand customers. This is less so in France and Japan, where a marketing strategy tends to be more intuitive, subjective, and less based on measured data.
- For a startup in the United States, especially in the early stage, it is essential to be optimistic, very confident, and to show your passion. This can be challenging to understand in France or in Japan, where it is common for people to express their doubts and show less confidence. In the United States, confidence and passion are critical to convincing investors and as morale boosters to recruited employees.

- Entrepreneurs coming from France and Japan tend to be technology-focused instead of market- and customer-driven, while in the United States, business and customers tend to be at the center of the creation of new opportunities.
- While in the United States and Europe starting with only a vision and abstract concepts is the norm, in a country like Japan, tangibility is king. Prototypes speak volumes, and concrete details are necessary to be convincing.
- In the United States, the art of pitching is practiced extensively as compellingly communicating ideas is an essential part of fundraising. It can be surprising for people coming from Europe or Asia, where there is not as much exigence and rigor on this method of communication.
- France and Japan are much more homogeneous countries than the United States, especially when compared to California's West Coast and other highly educated areas. The diversity present in some regions of the United States like Silicon Valley is an essential factor contributing to successful innovations.

Though these examples illustrate my experiences in France and Japan as compared to those in the United States, working with entrepreneurs from many different countries in Europe and Asia leads me to believe that, for the most part, they can be somewhat generalized to many other countries in Europe and Asia.

## 11.6. DISCOVERING USER EXPERIENCE

Having worked on technology (speech recognition and machine learning) for most of my career, when I started the innovation capabilities of Panasonic in Silicon Valley, I felt that the approach to create new business opportunities needed to change. Though the focus of Panasonic at the time was very much on technology to initiate new business creation, I felt that taking advantage of the Silicon Valley ecosystem was essential to create speed and that building a collaborative innovation model could help us do this. I also realized that we needed to focus more on the customer to figure out the directions to pursue. It is at this time that I explored design thinking with Stanford University, a pioneer in this area. This focus on design thinking brought us closer to understanding customer problems and helped us discover the importance of user experience.

User experience is crucial as it relates directly to user needs. *Figure 11.2* shows the user attributes of excellent user experience. Successful user experience provides positive experiences that consider the customer journey, leading to customer success. Our first success in this area came from the design of a new remote control called EZTouch, which featured two clickable touchpads feeding the sensor information to a TV-based user interface. At the time it was very revolutionary, and it received the "Best in Show" award at CEATEC in Japan (the equivalent of the CES show in the United States). This new remote control benefited from users' feedback incorporated in the design loop, validating at each step new prototypes developed very quickly. At CEATEC, the press reported that it was one of the first times that they were seeing a Japanese company innovating in a way similar to Apple. This success helped to push design thinking, rapid prototyping, and customer-based approaches inside Panasonic and legitimized user-centered innovation versus purely technology-based innovation.

However, user experience is different for everyone and difficult to measure. For Japanese companies which excel at developing optimized hardware and measuring progress and quality at every step, this was a departure. It was also tough for engineers not to assume that they knew what the users they were developing for needed and that users and customers were the ones to teach the company what they needed to create. In the end, slowly but surely, listening, observing, and questioning customers took a more central place inside the innovation process. It takes time to change the mindset and approach of a large corporation, and small successes along the way, such as EZTouch, are contributing to the need for change.

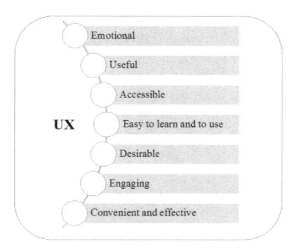

*Figure 11.2: Attributes of excellent user experience.*

## 11.7. SPINNING-IN A STARTUP INSIDE A CORPORATION

We all know what a corporate spin-off is, a startup originating within the corporation that separates from the corporation. Spinning-in is the process of creating this startup within the corporation. In the quest of searching for new business and the difficulties to go beyond incremental improvements by linking with internal business units, we began to incubate new opportunities in North America and push the boundaries of a traditional innovation lab by validating with potential customers and the market some of the new business opportunities discovered. One of these opportunities was related to the use of technology to help seniors be more socially engaged and keep their independence. This opportunity, called On4Today, started by using technology to compensate for the short-term memory loss of a person living in an assisted living facility. Later on, the solution addressed the problem of loneliness and social engagement by using technology to help increase the social aspects of their life, as older adults tend to withdraw as they age. It was a typical example of a problem-first approach where the opportunity started by solving a problem and transformed into a business opportunity.

After building a prototype, a video was made to highlight the benefits of the solution with testimonies from the different stakeholders. This video was very instrumental in going to the next step and getting internal corporate support to pursue the project. It was a powerful reminder that in the early stage, focusing on communicating the value proposition effectively instead of focusing on solely improving the technology can be a powerful approach to get to the next step.

The solution was piloted with several assisted living facilities and continuously improved with the help of many users. Then, the decision was made to pursue the effort and bring it to market. To bring it to market, more experimentation was needed to tune the business model and tune the value proposition to create a product-market fit. It is something that large corporations are not accustomed to, as experimenting with the market—up to gathering evidence of the customer's willingness to pay—is still not well accepted. Instead, large corporations pull the trigger by making a faith-based investment with insufficient product-market fit evidence, hoping that the massive market they wished for will become a reality. Furthermore, this internal startup was placed inside a sales division to go to market, emphasizing the pressure for ROI instead of tuning the product-market fit. Ultimately, On4Today went to market but did not yield the expected sales, and the project stopped though it initiated the creation of a new business unit in the area of Health and Wellness. This is an excellent example of the missing link between the front-end and the back-end of innovation, and of the lack of an end-to-end vision about how to create a new business opportunity. While the customer needs that the opportunity highlighted were clear (other startups and larger companies are pursuing a similar business area today), the corporation applied some traditional methods to develop/execute it, abandoning too early the needs for experimentation with the market. Furthermore, too much emphasis was placed too soon on ROI. There was also a minimal emphasis on learning as it was more a one-time shot instead of a longer-term approach to creating a sustainable new business creation process. Nevertheless, the execution of the opportunity up to the market introduction showed that the corporation was willing to try a new approach, even if it is likely to take several similar trials to get it right. Experimenting and continuously learning at every step of the opportunity development should guide new business creation, while the focus on ROI should take place when there is a convincing product-market fit.

## 11.8. THE LEADERSHIP TEAM IS THE STARTUP'S MOST CRUCIAL PIECE OF THE PUZZLE

Working with many startups for quite a few years helped me to appreciate how critical the leadership team (often it is the founding team) is to successful execution. Without exception, the leadership of the company was directly responsible for the successes or failures of the company. The primary reasons startups could not execute well include:

- Poor compatibility between the founders which led one of the founders to jump ship. It is a big issue as it destabilizes the startup. Unless a replacement is found quickly for the founder who leaves, it can be deadly for the startup.
- Not enough entrepreneurship expertise or business/strategy experience. To succeed a startup needs to have an experienced entrepreneur as a part of the leadership team. This is the person who makes things happen. The leadership team should also include a business-savvy leader who can articulate the business strategy together with an innovator who is supervising the product/service development. The innovator is often present. Finding these three areas of expertise in one person is atypical, as several members of the leadership team usually cover them. Experience shows that many startups lack an entrepreneur or a business-savvy leader, especially for startups that begin with the technology and try to create a new business leveraging the technology they developed.
- The founder has been successful in the past, made enough money to retire, and does not have the urge or the availability

to dedicate enough time and energy to the new venture. A startup cannot be a part-time job, and the leadership team needs to be fully committed to being successful.

- Inadequate execution expertise leading to low predictability and often overselling a vision which doesn't materialize in time. This is generally the case when the innovator is one of the most influential startup leaders.

Having experienced these situations through different startups made me understand that one of the essential criteria for VCs to invest in a startup is to evaluate whether the team has the necessary expertise and can execute or not. VCs expect that the plan will change and that the product that the startup will end up with is likely to be different from the one developed during the early stage of the startup. If the team is not strong, not complementary enough, or includes personalities that are difficult to work with, it will be difficult for the startup to deal successfully with the challenges that it will encounter. It is during these challenges that the team tends to fall apart.

## 11.9. YOUR NETWORK BECOMES A PART OF WHO YOU ARE

When I came to Silicon Valley, I realized that the way to innovate was quite different in this ecosystem as compared to the places I worked before, within the United States and outside. A lot of gatherings and events get organized every day. It is easy to get advice and to meet people who have the same passion as yourself. Furthermore, people are willing to help and share with you what they are doing. This networking model is one of the unique characteristics of the Silicon Valley ecosystem.

As an engineer by training, initially, I was not used to reaching out, and to exchanging and collaborating with people I just met. However, I quickly realized that by sharing my concerns, my challenges, and what I wanted to do, I could learn faster and discover new opportunities that did not even cross my mind. It became clear that I did not need to have all the pieces of the puzzle to be able to explore opportunities, and that I could figure out things along the way as long as I was passionate enough about the problem I wanted to solve and had a strong will to go forward.

As I evolved in this environment, I began to be much more externally focused, putting more emphasis on making things happen without worrying too much, at least initially, about having all the know-how and the resources to do it. It led me toward the area of open innovation where I became skilled at bringing in expertise and human resources just in time when we needed it. Progressively, I also connected to like-minded people that I could help, and that could help me. Networking tools such as LinkedIn, meetups, and area-focused events helped me tremendously to create a community that I could reach out to when necessary.

Over the years it became very apparent to me that building a network of people you have something in common with is not about reaching out to them only when you have some needs, but it is about creating a community of people that can help each other when needed. Many times, I connected to some individuals because there was something that made us do it, but I did not have any idea what this connection could bring in the future. However, at some point when a need arose, this past connection came back to my mind, and I reached out. A network or a community of people you connected with is a way to enlarge your space of possibilities and provide you options. This network is becoming the space you are evolving in when issues, challenges, or opportunities come up. It is becoming a part of who you are and it functions as an extension of yourself.

## 11.10. I ENJOYED THE RIDE, AND I AM STILL ENJOYING IT!

I started as a technologist in computer science with a focus on pattern recognition and speech processing. During more than 15 years, I enjoyed pushing the boundaries of speech recognition, writing many papers and patents, and participating in the growth of this area and the community associated with it. I also enjoyed integrating this technology into consumer products, though, at that time, speech recognition was more of a technology looking for an application and a market which could benefit from more data and computing power. Today, it is a much more mature technology pushed to the forefront of user interface technologies because of the higher recognition rates in real environments which are enabled by the data availability, the computational power available, and neural network models that can take better advantage of the large volume of data that is feeding these networks.

As a researcher and a passionate scientist looking for innovative ways to make an impact, from 2006, when I came to Silicon Valley, I became very interested in business models, business strategy and solving customer problems with technology. It opened my eyes as I realized that technology was only a means to solve problems. I am grateful to Stanford and the Center of Design Research led by Professor Larry Leifer for the help and guidance I received to appreciate the benefits of working with real problems and extracting and making sense of observations obtained from users in their natural environments to find insights. At the time, I loved this open space to find seeds of innovation instead of focusing on a particular technology and trying to figure out its domain of application.

This quest for creating new opportunities brought me into the startup world, first with an internal venture created inside Panasonic to help seniors be more independent and socially engaged, and later on with many startups across the world where I could apply my skills, help them grow and find their way. There is a saying that goes like this "It is hard to survive in a jungle if you were trained in a zoo." This is somewhat what I felt when I transitioned from a big corporation to the startup world, but as time went by, I felt more and more comfortable. Now I can say that I enjoy it very much, as for me it is always learning at a quick pace, and I love learning. Throughout the years, I had many failures and a few things I did well, but all the failures always motivated me to push forward and to leverage them to do better in the future.

I am still very much enjoying living in the fast lane and giving back to the young entrepreneurs who are discovering innovation and startup life. I wanted to write this book to share my experience with these young entrepreneurs and to tell them to never stop learning, to pursue their dreams though they may be hard to reach, to never give up their hopes, and to continue to work hard to make a difference in this world. By combining purpose and passion, I believe that we have the power to change the world!

# References

Adeeb, R. (2018, October 6). Retrieved from https://medium.com/@ramyadeeb/everything-you-should-know-about-the-new-post-money-safe-agreement-e90f09b9d3a8

Bengio, Y. (2009). *Learning Deep Architectures for AI*. Now Publishers Inc.

Blank, S. (2009, May 18). Retrieved from https://steveblank.com/2009/05/18/founders-and-dysfunctional-families/

Blank, S. (2011, March 31). Retrieved from https://steveblank.com/2011/03/31/entrepreneurship-is-an-art-not-a-job/

Blank, S. (2011, July 27). Retrieved from https://venturebeat.com/2011/07/27/entrepreneurship-is-an-art-not-a-job/

Blank, S. (2015, December 8). Retrieved from https://steveblank.com/2015/12/08/the-six-critical-decisions-to-make-before-establishing-an-innovation-outpost/

Blank, S., & Dorf, B. (2012). *The Startup Owner's Manual*. K&S Ranch, Inc.

Brown, B., & Anthony, S. D. (2011). How P&G Tripled Its Innovation Success Rate. *Harvard Business Review*.

Brown, T. (2019). *Change by Design: How Design Thinking Transforms Organizations and Inspires Innovation (Revised and Updated)*. Harper Business.

CB_Insights. (2018, February 2). Retrieved from https://www.cbinsights.com/research/startup-failure-reasons-top/

Chesbrough, H. (2003). *Open Innovation: The New Imperative for Creating and Profiting from Technology*. Harvard Business Review Press.

Chesbrough, H. (2006). *Open Business Models*. Harvard Business School Press.

Chesbrough, H. (2011). *Open Services Innovation*. Jossey-Bass, a Wiley Imprint.

Chesbrough, H., Vanhaverbeke, W., & West, J. (2006). *Open Innovation: Researching a New Paradigm*. Oxford University Press.

Cordon, C., & Nie, W. (2011, October). Retrieved from https://www.imd.org/research-knowledge/articles/leverage-the-supply-chain-to-improve-your-companys-bottom-line/

Cremades, A. (2016). *The Art of Startup Fundraising: Pitching Investors, Negotiating the Deal, and Everything Else Entrepreneurs Need to Know*. Wiley.

Diamandis, P. H. (2012). *Abundance: The Future Is Better Than You Think*. Free Press.

Duckworth, A. (2016). *Grit: The Power of Passion and Perseverance*. PCC.

Gibbs, S. (2014, December). Retrieved from https://www.theguardian.com/technology/2014/dec/03/google-glass-review-curiously-useful-overpriced-socially-awkward

Gioeli, A. (2014). *International Business Expansion: A Step-by-Step Guide to Launch Your Company Into Other Countries*. Over And Above Press .

Graham, P. (2009, October). Retrieved from http://www.paulgraham.com/really.html

Herbert, L. (2017). *Digital Transformation: Build Your Organization's Future for the Innovation Age*. Bloomsbury Business.

Humble, J., Molesky, J., & O'Reilly, B. (2015). *Lean Enterprise*. O'Reilly Media, Inc.

Humphrey, E. (2018, July 11). Retrieved from https://www.fpa-trends. com/article/rolling-forecast-philosophy-time-abandon-budget

Jensen, K. R. (2017). *Leading Global Innovation: Facilitating Multicultural Collaboration and International Market Success*. Palgrave Macmillan;.

Junqua, J.-C. (2000). *Robust Speech Recognition in Embedded Systems and PC Applications*. Kluwer Academic Publishers.

Junqua, J.-C., & Haton, J.-P. (1996). *Robustness in Automatic Speech Recognition*. Kluwer Academic Publishers.

Khosla, V. (2014, September 2). Retrieved from Khosla Ventures: https://www.khoslaventures.com/techcrunch-the-case-for-intelligent-failure-to-invent-the-future

LeCun, Y., Bengio, Y., & Hinton, G. (2015). Deep learning. *Nature, 521*, 436-444.

Lee, K.-F. (2018). *AI Superpowers: China, Silicon Valley, and the New World Order*. Houghton Mifflin Harcourt.

Liedtka, J., & Ogilvie, T. (2011). *Designing for Growth: a design thinking tool kit for managers*. Columbia Business School Publishing.

McChesney, C., Covey, S., & Huling, J. (2012). *The 4 Disciplines of Execution*. Free Press.

McChesney, C., Covey, S., & Huling, J. (2012). *The 4 Disciplines of Execution*. FrankingCovey Co.

McKinsey Global Institute. (2017). *Jobs Lost, Jobs Gained: Workforce Transitions in a Time of Automation*. McKinsey&Company.

Miles, R. E. (2005). *Collaborative Entrepreneurship: How Communities of Networked Firms Use Continuous Innovation to Create Economic Wealth*. Stanford University Press.

Moore, G. A. (2014). *Crossing the Chasm, 3rd edition*. HarperCollins Publishers.

Norman, A. T. (2017). *Blockchain Technology Explained: The Ultimate Beginner's Guide About Blockchain Wallet, Mining, Bitcoin, Ethereum, Litecoin, Zcash, Monero, Ripple, Dash, IOTA And Smart Contracts*. CreateSpace Independent Publishing Platform.

O'Donnell, C., & Franklin, J. (2019, March 17). Retrieved from https://www.reuters.com/article/us-lyft-ipo/lyft-to-launch-road-show-for-up-to-2-billion-ipo-sources-idUSKCN1QY08D

O'Reilly III, C. A., & Tushman, M. L. (2004). The Ambidextrous Organization. *Harvard Business Review.*

O'Reilly, B. (2019). *Unlearn: Let Go of Past Success to Achieve Extraordinary Results.* McGraw Hill Digital.

Osterwalder, A., & Pigneur, Y. (2010). *Business Model Generation.* Self Published.

Osterwalder, A., Pigneur, Y., Bernarda, G., & Smith, A. (2014). *Value Proposition Design.* Wiley.

Plattner, H., Meinel, C., & Leifer, L. (2010). *Design thinking: understand–improve–apply.* Springer Science & Business Media.

Poland, S. R. (2014). *Founder's Pocket Guide: Startup Valuation .* 1x1 Media.

Reichheld, F. F. (2003, December). The One Number You Need to Grow. *Harvard Business Review.* Retrieved from https://hbr.org/2003/12/the-one-number-you-need-to-grow

Riani, A. (2017, February 4). Retrieved from Why Is Starting Startups So Hard?

Ries, E. (2011). *The Lean Startup: How Today's Entrepreneurs Use Continuous Innovation to Create Radically Successful Businesses.* Currency.

Savoia, A. (2019). *The Right It: Why So Many Ideas Fail and How to Make Sure Yours Succeed.* HarperOne.

Stegmaier, J. (2015). *A Crowdfunder's Strategy Guide: Build a Better Business by Building Community.* Berrett-Koehler Publishers.

Stretch, J. (2012). *Managing with rolling forecasts v2.* Stretch Publishing.

Verganti, R. (2009). *Design-Driven Innovation.* Harvard Business School Publishing Corporation.

Weinberg, G., & Mares, J. (2015). *Traction: How Any Startup Can Achieve Explosive Customer Growth.* Penguin Random House LLC.

Winfrey, G. (2014, June 13). Retrieved from https://www.inc.com/graham-winfrey/peter-diamandis-billion-dollar-problems.html

# Index